LESLEY DUNCAN, a history graduat
and the State University of Pennsy...., ..., ...,
poetry editor of *The Herald* newspaper, Glasgow. She also writes
poetry herself, much of it on contemporary events and issues,
and is joint editor with Maurice Lindsay of the *Edinburgh Book
of Twentieth-Century Scottish Poetry* (Edinburgh University
Press, 2005).

ELSPETH KING is the Director of the Stirling Smith Art Gallery
and Museum, which has a large collection of Wallace memora-
bilia. She introduced and edited the Luath Press edition of *Blind
Harry's Wallace*, published in 1998. In 1997 the Smith hosted the
exhibition *Scotland's Liberator – The Life and Legacy of William
Wallace* to mark the 700th anniversary of the Battle of Stirling
Bridge; in 2005 the Smith hosts *The Face of William Wallace* exhi-
bition to commemorate the 700th anniversary of his execution.

The Wallace Muse

Poems and artworks inspired by the life
and legend of William Wallace

Poetry selected by
Lesley Duncan

Artworks selected by
Elspeth King

Luath Press Limited

EDINBURGH

www.luath.co.uk

For permission to reprint poems in copyright, thanks are due to the poets and/or to the following:

'The Guairdian Wallace' and 'The Martyr' by T.S. Law reproduced by kind permission of John Law.

'William Wallace at Westminster, 1305' by James S. Adam from *The Scots Glasnost*, Issue 8, 1993.

'1305' by Geddes Thomson from *Four Scottish Poets*, Garron Publications, 1983 reproduced by kind permission of Mrs Lucy Thomson.

'The Wallace' by Sydney Goodsir Smith from *The Wallace: a triumph in five acts*, Calder Publications Limited, 1985.

'Braveheart!' by David Kinloch from *Un Tour d' Ecosse*, Carcanet Press Ltd, 2001.

'Barnweil Hill, by Craigie' by Gordon Jarvie from *The Ayrshire Recessional*, Harpercroft Press, 1998.

'Receiving a Traitor's Leg, Perth, 1305' by Fergus Chadwick from *Chapman*, vol. 63, Spring 1991.

All artworks reproduced by kind permission of The Trustees of Stirling Smith Art Gallery and Museum.

Contents

Introduction

THIS BOOK DRAWS together a fascinatingly diverse collection of poetry about the Scottish patriot Sir William Wallace; the 700th anniversary of his death falls this year. It ranges from Blind Harry's great epic poem written in the 1470s to a contemporary reflection written especially for this publication by Edwin Morgan, Scotland's official poet, or Makar.

For 700 years William Wallace has had an extraordinary hold on the Scottish psyche. Centuries of subsequent national history – the retrieval of Scottish independence under the ambivalent figure of Robert the Bruce at Bannockburn, the upheaval of the Reformation, the Unions of Crown and Parliament, Jacobite uprisings, industrial and social revolutions, and two World Wars – have not dimmed Wallace's grip on the Scottish imagination. That grip is all the more impressive in view of his barbaric execution in London in 1305 at the hands of Edward 1. Heroes do not, as a rule, end up disembowelled and with their dismembered limbs displayed prominently throughout the land to discourage followers. In spite of that dreadful fate, Wallace has always surmounted the role of martyr to be seen as the true enabler of Scottish independence; the quintessential champion of Scotland and of ordinary Scots; and indeed iconic figure of freedom and liberty in an even wider context.

Wallace's international reputation certainly predated Mel Gibson's simplistic heroics in the Hollywood film *Braveheart*. The Italian patriots Garibaldi and Mazzini were among the supporters of the National Wallace Monument erected in Stirling in the 1860s by public subscription. Garibaldi's glowing tribute concluded with these words: 'William Wallace,

Scotland's noblest hero, sheds as bright a glory upon his valorous nation as ever was shed upon their country by the greatest men of Greece and Rome.'

Tantalisingly little is certain about Wallace's life. Even his reputed birthplace in Elderslie, Renfrewshire, is disputed. The pivotal moment in his life, when his wife or sweetheart – variously named Marion, Mirren, and even Fidelia in different accounts – was murdered by the English Sheriff of Lanark, is also shrouded in conjecture. What is definitely known of Wallace is that he galvanised resistance to the English after Edward I exploited the dispute over the vacant Scottish crown to claim sovereignty over Scotland; that he had a decisive victory against the English at the Battle of Stirling Bridge in 1297; became Guardian of Scotland; lost the Battle of Falkirk the following year, partly at least because of the defection of the Scottish nobility including Robert the Bruce; spent some years in France; and was finally betrayed by Sir John Menteith and handed over to the English for trial and execution in 1305.

This spare but momentous framework of a life has generated much poetry to commemorate it. First to tackle the subject was the mysterious Blind Harry whose epic poem was written in the 1470s and first published in 1508. Harry claimed that his work was based on a contemporary life of Wallace written by his confessor Blair, though that book, if it ever existed, has disappeared from history. His narrative draws on myth as well as fact. The late medieval Scots language which Harry employs is difficult for today's readers, but there is no doubt about his literary flair, the scope of his vision, or the vigour of his narrative; Wallace is shown smiting an extraordinary number of English in apparently endless skirmishes as well as larger battles.

The whole poem is indeed very anti-English in sentiment

– a characteristic that was maintained by William Hamilton of Gilbertfield in his reworking of the narrative in 1722. This was the version of the Wallace story known to Burns, and indeed the Hamilton volume was, next to the Bible, the most popular book in Scotland in the eighteenth century. Some of the most stirring lines from Burns's *Scots Wha Hae* are lifted almost directly from Hamilton's re-telling of the Battle of Biggar. The inspiration provided by Wallace is woven into the fabric of Burns's writing and idealism.

William Wordsworth, himself a warm admirer of Burns, wrote a brief paean to Wallace in *The Prelude*. His fellow Lake Poet, Robert Southey, also wrote sympathetically about the Scottish hero, as did Thomas Campbell, author of *Ye Mariners of England* (although Campbell was a Glaswegian by birth). Robert Tannahill, the Paisley weaver-poet, and the irrepressible William McGonagall both penned poems about him, as did other lesser known versifiers, inspired by a resurgence of patriotic emotion in Victorian times. These are all represented in this book, as are traditional, anonymous ballads that Wallace inspired. The hold that Wallace had on Scots of the Caledonian diaspora is also proved by extracts from an extraordinary hand-written epic poem composed by Andrew Munro in Brooklyn, New York over a period of 36 years in the late nineteenth century.

The Wallace Muse also offers modern poems on the theme of Wallace. Edwin Morgan leads a distinguished group of contemporary Scottish writers. Les Murray, the much admired Australian poet, has written a piece for the anthology, and there are extracts from two plays about Wallace, taken from Sydney Goodsir Smith's *The Wallace*, which was part of the official Edinburgh Festival programme in 1960, and from John Fowler's revisionist *Whaur's Yer Willie Wallace Noo?*, dating from 1976.

Wallace has not only inspired poets and writers – his legend and legacy has also been left to the visual arts. For this reason, *The Wallace Muse* includes a colour photograph section with details of the paintings, statues, book covers and other artworks that have depicted and been inspired by William Wallace over the years, from the second-oldest portrait of him in existence through to contemporary book covers and illustrations, many selected by Elspeth King, Director of the Stirling Smith Art Gallery and Museum, from the Smith's past and present exhibitions of Wallace images and memorabilia.

Not all of the material is laudatory. Some poems ponder, if implicitly, the ambivalent nature of patriotism: how one man's freedom fighter may be another's terrorist. Wallace's capacity for cruelty as well as nobility is examined. Whatever his motivation and ultimate personal tragedy, Wallace remains a potent myth for Scots. I hope that the range of poems offered here will shed new insights not just into the man himself and his extraordinary times, but into his inspirational hold on his compatriots throughout the succeeding centuries. The poetry is also simply to be enjoyed in its own right.

Lesley Duncan
Stirling, August 2005

Lines for Wallace

Edwin Morgan

*Scotland's official poet responds with a passionate eloquence
to Wallace's story, reflecting that, 'The power of Wallace/ Cuts
through art/ But art calls attention to it/ Badly or well.'*

Is it not better to forget?
It is better not to forget.
Betrayal never to be forgotten,
Vindictiveness never to be forgotten,
Triumphalism never to be forgotten.
Body parts displayed
At different points of the compass,
Between hanging and hacking
The worst, the disembowelling.
Blood raised in him, fervent,
Blood raced in him, fervent,
Blood razed in him, for ever
Fervent in its death.
For Burns was right to see
It was not only in the field
That Scots would follow this man
With blades and war-horns
Sharp and shrill
But with brains and books
Where the idea of liberty
Is impregnated and impregnates.

Oh that too is sharp and shrill
And some cannot stand it
And some would never allow it
And some would rather die
For the regulated music
Of Zamyatin's Polyhymnia
Where nothing can go wrong.
Cinema sophisticates
Fizzed with disgust at the crudities
Braveheart held out to them.
Over the cheeks of some
(Were they less sophisticated?)
A tear slipped unbidden.
Oh yes it did. I saw it.
The power of Wallace
Cuts through art
But art calls attention to it
Badly or well.
In your room, in the street
Even by god if it came to it,
On a battlefield,
Think about it,
Remember him.

Part One

Poems inspired by Wallace: 15th – 19th centuries

Blind Harry's Wallace

Blind Harry (c.1440–c.1493)

*The opening section of the original Blind Harry epic, dating
from the 1470s, contrasted with the same section in the 1722
text shows how much language had evolved in the two and a
half centuries, and also the way Hamilton reworked and rein-
terpreted the original material. From the start an anti-English
tone is set, but while Harry refers only to the Saxons, Hamilton
adds Picts and Danes to the list of 'Scotland's very pest.'*

Our antecessowris that we suld of reide
And hald in mynde thar nobille worthi deid,
We lat ourslide throu verray sleuthfulnes,
And castis us ever till uther besynes.
Till honour ennymyis is our haile entent:
It has beyne seyne in thir tymys bywent.
Our ald ennemys cummyn of Saxonys blud,
That nevyr yeit to Scotland wald do gud
Bot ever on fors and contrar haile thar will,
Quhow gret kyndnes thar has beyne kyth thaim till.
It is weyle knawyne on mony divers syde
How thai haff wrocht in to thar mychty pryde
To hald Scotlande at undyr evermar,
Bot God abuff has maid thar mycht to par.
Yhit we suld thynk one our bearis befor;
Of thar parablys as now I say no mor.
We reide of ane rycht famous of renowne,
Of worthi blude that ryngis in this regioune,
And hensfurth I will my proces hald
Of Wilyham Wallas yhe haf hard beyne tald.

William Hamilton of Gilbertfield's version

Of our ancestors, brave true ancient Scots,
Whose glorious scutcheons knew no bars nor blots;
But blood untainted circled ev'ry vein,
And ev'ry thing ignoble did disdain;
Of such illustrious patriots and bold,
Who stoutly did maintain our rights of old,
Who their malicious, and invet'rate foes,
With sword in hand, did gallantly oppose:
And in their own, and nation's just defence,
Did briskly check the frequent insolence
Of haughty neighbours, enemies profest,
Picts, Danes, and Saxons, Scotland's very pest;
Of such, I say, I'll brag and vaunt so long
As I have pow'r to use my pen or tongue;
And sound their praises in such modern strain,
    As suiteth best a Scot's poetic vein.
First, here I honour, in particular,
Sir William Wallace, much renown'd in war;
Whose bold progenitors have long time stood,
Of honourable and true Scottish blood...

Blind Harry's Wallace – Excerpt
regarding Wallace's Appearance

Blind Harry (c. 1440–1493)

As with other figures of that period in Scotland, there are no contemporary portraits to show the physical appearance of Wallace. The earliest depictions (rather gloomy and long-nosed) date from the seventeenth century. It is not at all obvious that the artists had referred to Blind Harry, who offers this vivid description of Wallace in Book 10 of his poem. Even when allowances are made for hyperbole, it is clear that Wallace was a most imposing figure. The size of his sword in Stirling's National Wallace Monument also testifies to his strength. Hamilton's interpretation of Harry's description is more accessible to modern readers.

Bot I hereof can nocht rehers thaim aw.
Wallace statur, of gretnes and of hycht,
Was jugyt thus be dyscrecioun of rycht,
That saw him bath dischevill and in weid.
Nine quartaris large he was in lenth indeid;
Thryd part that lenth in schuldrys braid was he,
Rycht sembly strang and lusty for to se;
Hys lymmys gret, with stalwart pais and sound,
Hys browys hard, his armes gret and round;
His handis maid rycht lik till a pawmer,
Of manlik mak, with nales gret and cler;
Proporcionyt lang and fair was his vesage,
Rycht sad of spech and abill in curage;
Braid breyst and heych with sturdy crag and gret,neck
His lyppys round, his noys was squar and tret;

Bowand bron haryt on browis and breis lycht,
Cler aspre eyn lik dyamondis brycht.
Under the chyn on the left sid was seyn
Be hurt a wain; his colour was sangweyn.
Woundis he had in mony divers place,
Bot fair and weill kepyt was his face.
Of ryches he kepyt no propyr thing,
Gaiff as he wan, like Alexander the king.
In tym of pes mek as a maid was he;
Quhar wer approchyt the rycht Ector was he.
To Scottis men a gret credens he gaiff,
Bot knawin enemys thai couth him nocht dissayff.

William Hamilton of Gilbertfield's version

The wits of France have with the herald sent,
A brave description, and a fine comment   description of
On Wallace's actions, and his person rare,   Wallace
To either which the age could not compare.
In stature he was full nine quarter high,
When measured, at least, without a lie.
Betwixt his shoulders was three quarters
      broad,
Such length and breadth would now a-days
      seem odd.
Was no fatigue but what he could endure;
Great, but well shaped limbs, voice strong
      and sture.
Burning brown hair, his brows and
      eye-bries light;   eyebrows
Quick piercing eyes, like to the diamonds
      bright.

A well proportion'd visage, long and sound;
Nose square and neat, with ruddy lips and round.
His breast was high, his neck was thick and strong;
A swinging hand, with arms both large and long.
Grave in his speech, his colour sanguine fine,
A beauteous face, wherein did honour shine.
In time of peace, mild as a lamb would be,
When war approach'd, a Hector stout was he.
Riches he mock'd, submitted all to fate;
Gave what he wan, like Alexander great.
To Scotsmen he great trust and credit gave,
But a known foe could never him deceive.
Such qualities, men did to him advance
Who were the very greatest wits in France...

Wallace – Excerpt in which Wallace is Visited in a Dream by King Fergus and Lady Fortune

William Hamilton of Gilbertfield (c.1665–1751)

Wallace gets his lofty marching orders from Fergus King of Scots and Dame Fortune. Hamilton has here played to post-Reformation sentiments by substituting King Fergus for St Andrew and Fortune for the Blessed Virgin. But the dream episode retains its visionary epic quality, with echoes even of Christ's temptation in the wilderness. And the eighteenth-century text still carries the implication of divine mission for Wallace's cause: 'Thou granted are by the great God above / To help and aid poor people that get wrong.' This text, perhaps above all others, shows the almost transcendental nature of Wallace's reputation.

He lean'd him down upon a place hard by,
Then in a deep sleep fell immediately:
Into that slumber Wallace thought he saw,
A stalwart man, that towards him did draw;
Who hastily did catch him by the hand;
'I am,' he said, 'sent to thee by command:'
A sword he gave him of the finest steel,
'This sword,' said he, 'son, may thou
    manage weel:'
A topaz fine, the plummet, did he guess,
The hilt and all did glitter o'er like glass.
'Dear son,' said he, 'we tarry here too long;
Shortly thou must revenge thy country's
    wrong.'

Then led he him unto a mountain high,
Where he at once all the world might see;
Where left he Wallace, contrair his desire,
To whom appear'd a very dreadful fire,
Which fiercely burnt and wasted through
    the land.
Scotland all o'er, from Ross to Solway sand.
Quickly to him descended there a queen,
All shining bright, and with majestic mein:
Her countenance did dazzle so his sight,
It quite extinguish'd all the fire light.
Of red and green gave him, with modest grace,
A wand, and with a sapphire cross'd   She makes the sign
    his face.   of the saltire on
                                                  his face.
'Welcome,' she said, 'I choose thee for my
    love,
Thou granted art by the great God above,
To help and aid poor people that get wrong,
But with thee now I must not tarry long:
To thine own host thou shalt return again,
Thy dearest kin in torment are and pain.
This kingdom, thou redeem it surely shall,
Though thy reward on earth shall be but
    small.
Go on and prosper, sure thou shalt not
    miss,
For thy reward, the heaven's eternal bliss.'
With her right hand, she reached him a
    book,
Then hastily her leave of him she took.
Unto the clouds ascended out of sight.
Wallace the book embrac'd with all his
    might.
The book was writ in three parts, and no
    less

25

The first big letters were and all of brass
The second gold, silver the third most fine,
At which he greatly wondered in his mind:
To read the book he made great haste, but as
He did awake, behold a dream it was.
Quickly he rose, and there a man he found,
Who did his dream and vision all expound.
'The stalwart man, who gave thee that
    fine sword.
Was Fergus King of Scots, upon my word.
The mountain does prognosticate no less
Than knowledge how our wrongs thou
    must redress.
The fire hasty tidings doth presage,
The like of which was not heard in our age.
The bright and shining queen, whom thou
    didst see,
Was Fortune, which portends great good
    to thee.
The pretty wand which she unto thee sent,
Betokens power, command, and
    chastisement.
The colour red, if I rightly understand,
Means bloody battles shortly in our land.
The green, great courage to thee does portend,
And trouble great, before the wars shall end.
The sapphire stone, she blessed thee withal,
Is happy chance; pray God it thee befall.
The threefold book, is this poor broken land,
Thou must redeem by thy most valiant hand.
The great big letters which thou saw of brass,
Prognostic wars, that shall this land oppress.
Yet every thing to its true right again,

In Harry's original, the sword bearer is St Andrew

Harry's original identifies her as the Blessed Virgin.

26

Thou shalt restore; but thou must suffer pain.
The gold betokens honour, worthiness,
Victorious arms, manhood, and nobleness.
The silver shows clean life, and heavenly bliss,
Which thou worthy reward shalt never miss.
Then do not fear, or in the least despair,
He shall protect thee who of all takes care.'

Wallace – The Battle of Biggar

William Hamilton of Gilbertfield (c.1665–1751)

In the Hamilton text, this battle takes place after both the murder of Fidelia, Wallace's wife, by Hasilrig, the Sheriff of Lanark, and Wallace's revenge killing of the murderer. Its vivid description of the battlefield resonates with phrases and emotions that were to inspire Burns's Scots Wha Hae: '*A false usurper sinks in ev'ry foe,/ And liberty returns with every blow.' The battle itself may not be historical.*

Now Biggar's plains with armed men are crown'd,
And shining lances glitter all around;
The sounding horn and clarions all conspire
To raise the soldier's breast, and kindle up his fire.
The hero tir'd of Lanark's luckless land,
Swift now to Biggar leads his conqu'ring band:
Each heaving breast with thirst of vengeance glows,
And in their tow'ring hopes already slay their foes.
The careful warrior on a rising ground
Encamp'd, and saw the dreadful foes around,
Stretch'd out in wide array along the plain,
And in his heart biggens with the glorious scene.
    But now the morning in fair beams arrayed,
Rose on the dark, and chased the nightly shade,
Each eager soldier seized his ready shield,
Draws the fierce blade, and strides along the field;
In black'ning wings extends from left to right;
Condense in war, and gather to the fight;
Thick beats each heart, waiting the least command

And death stands lingering in the lifted hand.
Wallace then threw around his skilful eyes,
And saw with joy their eager passions rise.
'To day, my friends, to day let's boldly dare
Each doubtful hazard of the uncertain war;
Let our fierce swords be deeply drench'd in gore,
And then our toils and labour shall be o'er.
See! round our heads the guardian angels stand,
And guide the javelin in each eager hand;
To Edward shall they bear the flying dart,
And with the pointed javelin pierce his heart.
Let glorious liberty each soul inspire,
Raise every heart, and rouse the warrior's fire.'
He said, and kindling into fury rose each breast.
With love of virtue all at once possess'd;
Eager they thicken on the mountain's brow
And hang impendent on the plain below.
The foe, surpris'd, look up and see from far.
The progress of the swift descending war;
They run, they fly, in ranks together close.
And in a steely circle meet their coming foes.
But now the Scottish heroes bend their way,
Where in his tent the royal monarch lay;
There rose the battle, there the warriors tend,
A thousand deaths on thousand wings ascend;
Swords, shields, and spears in mix'd confusion glow.
The field is swept, and lessens at each blow.
Wallace's helm distinguish'd from afar,
Tempests the field, and floats amid'st the war;
Imperious death attends upon his sword,
And certain conquest waits her destin'd lord.
Fierce in another quarter Kent employs

The wrathful spear, nor fewer foes destroys;
Where'er he conquering turns, recedes the foe,
And thickened troops fly open to his blows;
His bounding courser thundering o'er the plain
Bears his fierce rapid lord o'er hills of slain;
Scarce can the weak retreating Scots withstand
The mighty sweep of the invader's hand.
Wallace beheld his fainting squadron yield,
And various slaughter spread along the field,
Furious he hastes, and heaves his orbed shield
Resolv'd in arms to meet his enemy.
Before his spear they rush, they run, they fly.
And now in equal battle meet the foes.
Long lasts the combat, and resound their blows:
Their dreadful faulchions brandishing on high.   broadswords
In wavy circles heighten to the sky;
With furious ire they run the field around,
And keen on death, explore each secret wound.
They heave, they pant, they beat in every vein,
While death sits idle on the crimson plain.
Long in suspense the uncertain battle hung,
And fortune, fickle goddess, doubted long
On whom she should the laurel wreath bestow,
Whom raise as conqueror, whom depress as foe.
At last the Hero, tir'd with forc'd delay,
At his full stretch rose, and with mighty sway,
Bore from the foe his shield's defence away.
Now high in the air the shiny sword he rear'd,
Ponderous with fate the shiny sword appear'd:
Descending full, it stops his stifled breath;
Giddy, he turns around, and reels in death.
The stringy nerves are wrapt around in gore,

And rushing blood distain'd his armour o'er.
Now all is death and wounds; the crimson plain
Floats round in blood, and groans beneath its slain.
Promiscuous crowds one common ruin share,
And death alone employs the wasteful war.
They trembling fly by conquering Scots oppress'd,
And the broad ranks of battle lie defac'd;
A false usurper sinks in ev'ry foe,
And liberty returns with every blow.

Sir William Wallace and The Gude Wallace

Anonymous traditional ballads

These two traditional ballads both seem to centre on the same episode from Blind Harry, when a woman Wallace was visiting (presumably for carnal reasons) repented about betraying him to the English soldiery and helped him to escape in her clothes. In the first, however, she seems conflated with his lover/sweetheart in Lanark.

Sir William Wallace

Wou'd ye hear of William Wallace,
    And seek him as he goes,
Into the land of Lanark,
    Amang his mortal foes?

There were fifteen English sogers
    Unto his ladye came,
Said, 'Gi'e us William Wallace,
    That we may have him slain.

'Wou'd ye gi'e William Wallace,
    That we may have him slain?
And ye'se be wedded to a lord,
    The best in Christendeem.'

'This very night, at seven
    Brave Wallace will come in,
And he'll come to my chamber door,
    Without or dread or din.'

The fifteen English sogers
    Around the house did wait;
And four brave Southron foragers
    Stood hie upon the gait.

That very night, at seven,
    Brave Wallace he came in,
And he came to his ladye's bow'r
    Withouten dread or din.

When she beheld brave Wallace,
    And stared him in the face –
'Ohon, alas:' said that ladye,
    'This is a woeful case.

'For I this night have sold you,
    This night you must be ta'en:
And I'm to be wedded to a lord,
    The best in Christendeem.'

'Do you repent,' said Wallace,
    'The ill you've done to me?'
'Ay, that I do,' said that ladye,
    'And will do till I dee.

'Ay, that I do,' said that ladye,
    'And will do ever still;
And for the ill I've done to you,
    Let me burn upon a hill.'
'Now, God forfend,' says brave Wallace,

'I should be so unkind;
Whatever I am to Scotland's faes,
    I'm aye a woman's friend.

'Will ye gi'e me your gown, your gown,
    Your gown but and your kirtle,
Your petticoat of bonnie brown,
    And belt about my middle?

'I'll take a pitcher in ilka hand,
    And do me to the well;
They'll think I'm one of your maidens,
    Or think it is yoursel'.'

She has gi'en him her gown, her gown,
    Her petticoat and kirtle;
Her broadest belt with silver clasps,
    To bind about his middle.

He's ta'en a pitcher in ilka hand,
    And done him to the well;
They thought him one of her maidens,
    They kenn'd 'twas not hersel'.

Said one of the Southron foragers,
    'See ye yon lusty dame?
I wou'd me gi'e meikle to thee, neebor,
    To bring her back again.'

Then all the Southron follow'd him,
    They follow'd him all four;
But he has drawn his trusty brand,
    And slain them pair by pair.

The Gude Wallace

Wallace wicht, upon a nicht,
    Cam riding ower a lin;
And he is to his leman's bouir,
    And tirl'd at the pin.

'O sleep ye, or wake ye, lady?' he cried;
    'Ye'll rise and let me in.'
'O wha is this at my bouir door,
    That knocks and knows my name?'
'My name is William Wallace;
    Ye may my errand ken.'

'The truth to you I will rehearse –
    The secret I'll unfauld;
Into your enemies' hands, this nicht,
    I fairly hae you sauld.'

'If that be true ye tell to me,
    Do ye repent it sair?'
'Oh, that I do,' she said, 'dear Wallace,
    And will do evermair!

The English did surround my house,
    And forcit me theretill;
But for your sake, my dear Wallace,
    I could burn on a hill.'

The he ga'e her a loving kiss;
    The teir drapt frae his ee;
Says, 'Fare ye weel for evermair;
    Your face nae mair I'll see.'

She dress'd him in her ain claithing,
    And frae her house he came;
Which made the Englishmen admire
    To see sic a stalwart dame!

Now Wallace to the Hielands went,
    Where nae meat nor drink had he;
Said, 'Fa' me life, or fa' me death,
    To some toun I maun drie.'

He steppit ower the river Tay –
    On the North Inch steppit he;
And there he saw a weel-faured May,   maiden
    Was waushing aneath a tree.

'What news, what news, ye weel-faured May?
    What news hae ye to me?
What news, what news, ye weel-faured May,
    What news in the south countrie?'

'O see ye, sir, yon hostler-house
    That stands on yonder plain?
This very day have landit in it
    Full fifteen Englishmen,

In search of Wallace, our champion,
    Intending he should dee!'
'Then, by my sooth,' says Wallace wicht,
    'These Englishmen I'se see.

If I had but in my pocket
    The worth of a single pennie,
I wad gang to the hostler-house,
    These gentlemen to see.'

She put her hand in her pocket,
    And pull'd out half-a-croun,
Says, 'Tak ye that, ye beltit knicht,
    Aud pay your lawin doun.'   reckoning

As he went frae the weel-faured May,
    A beggar bold met he,
Was cover'd wi' a clouted cloke,
    In his hand a trustie tree.

'What news, what news, ye silly auld man?
    What news hae ye to gie?'
'No news, no news, ye beltit knicht,
    No news hae I to thee,
But fifteen lords in the hostler-house
    Waiting Wallace for to see.'

'Ye'll lend to me your clouted cloke,
    That kivers ye frae heid to shie;
And I'll go to the hostler-house,
    To ask for some supplie.'

Now he's gane to the West-muir wood,
    And pulled a trustie trie;
And then he's on to the hostler gone,
    Asking there for charitie.

Doun the stair the captain comes,
    The puir man for to see:
'If ye be captain as gude as ye look,
    You'll give me some supplie.'

'Where were ye born, ye cruikit carle?
  Where, and in what countrie?
'In fair Scotland, sir, was I born,
  Cruikit carle as ye ca' me.'

'O I wad give you fifty pounds
  Of gold and white monie;
O I wad give you fifty pounds,
  If Wallace ye would let me see.'

'Tell doun your money,' quo' the cruikit carle,
  'Tell doun your money good;
I'm sure I have it in my pouir,
  And never had a better bode.'   offer

The money was told upon the table,
  Of silver pounds fiftie:
'Now here I stand!' quo' the gude Wallace,
  And his cloke frae him gar'd flie.

He slew the captain where he stood;
  The rest they did quake and rair:
He slew the rest around the room;
  Syne ask'd if there were ony mair.

'Get up, get up, gudewife,' he says,
  'And get me some dinner in haste;
For it soon will be three lang days time,
  Sin' a bit o' meat I did taste!'

The dinner was na weil readie,
  Nor yet on the table set,
When other fifteen Englishmen
  Were lichtit at the yett.   gate

'Come out, come out, thou traitor, Wallace!
    This is the day ye maun dee!'
'I lippen nae sae little to God,' he says,
    'Although I be but ill wordie.'

The gudewife had an auld gudeman;
    By gude Wallace he stiffly stude,
Till ten o' the fifteen Englishmen
    Lay before the door in their blude.

The other five he took alive,
    To the greenwood as they ran;
And he has hanged them, bot mercie,   *without mercy*
    Up hich upon a grain.   *a forked branch of a tree*

Now he is on to the North Inch gone,
    Where the May was washing tenderlie.
'Now, by my sooth,' said the gude Wallace,
    'It's been a sair day's wark to me.'

He's put his hand in his pocket,
    And pulled out twenty pounds;
Says, 'Take ye that, ye weel-faured May,
    For the gude luck o' your half-croun.'

Full five-and-twenty men he slew,
    Five hanged upon a grain;
On the morn he sat, wi' his merry-men a',
    In Lochmaben toun at dine.

Glorious Wallace – Excerpt from To William Simpson, Ochiltree

Robert Burns (1759 – 1796)

Robert Burns wrote that 'the story of Wallace poured a Scottish prejudice in my veins which will boil there until the floodgates of life shut in eternal rest.' Emotive sentiments, and indeed Wallace became a powerful leitmotif of his poetry, whether as the main subject or as a point of reference for thoughts on liberty and the Scottish nation and character in the context of Burns's own times. Guid Wallace *is the exception, looking back as it does to the traditional ballads and their tales of besting the English soldiery.*

We'll sing auld Coila's plains and fells,
Her moors red brown wi' heather bells,
Her banks an' braes, her dens an' dells,
    Where glorious WALLACE
Aft bure the gree, as story tells
      Frae Suthron billies.

At WALLACE' name, what Scottish Blood,
But boils up in a spring time flood!
Oft have our fearless fathers strode
    By WALLACE' side,
Still pressing onward, red-wat-shod,
      or glorious dy'd!

Scots Wha Hae
or **Robert Bruce's March to Bannockburn**

Robert Burns (1759—1796)

Scots wha hae wi' Wallace bled
Scots wham Bruce has aften led
Welcome to your gory bed
Or to victorie.
Now's the day and now's the hour
See the front o' battle lour
See approach proud Edward's power
Chains and slaverie.

Wha will be a traitor knave?
Wha can fill a coward's grave?
Wha sae base as be a slave?
Let him turn and flee.
Wha for Scotland's King and Law
Freedom's sword will strongly draw
Freeman stand or Freeman fa'
Let him follow me.

By Oppression's woes and pains
By your sons in servile chains
We will drain our dearest veins
But they shall be free.
Lay the proud Usurpers low
Tyrants fall in every foe
Liberty's in ever blow
Let us do or dee!

Excerpt from **The Cottar's Saturday Night**

Robert Burns (1759—1796)

O Thou! who pour'd the patriotic tide,
That stream'd thro Wallace's undaunted heart,
Who dar'd to nobly stem tyrannic pride,
Or nobly die, the second glorious part:
(The patriot's God peculiarly thou art,
His friend, inspirer, guardian, and reward!)
O never, never Scotia's realm desert;
But still the patriot, and the patriot-bard
In bright succession raise, her ornament and guard!

Excerpt from **Ode for General Washington's Birthday**

Robert Burns (1759—1796)

Thee, Caledonia, thy wild heaths among,
Fam'd for the martial deed, the heaven-taught song,
To thee I turn with swimming eyes!
Where is that soul of Freedom fled?
Immingled with the mighty dead
Beneath that hallow'd turf where WALLACE lies!
Hear it not, Wallace, in thy bed of death!
Ye babbling winds, in silence sweep!
Disturb not ye the hero's sleep,
Nor give the coward secret breath!
Is this the ancient Caledonian form,
Firm as her rock, resistless as her storm?
Show me that eye which shot immortal hate,
Blasting the Despot's proudest bearing!
Show me that arm which, nerv'd with thundering fate,
Braved Usurpation's boldest daring!
Dark-quench'd as yonder sinking star,
No more that glance lightens afar,
That palsied arm no more whirls on the waste of war.

Guid Wallace

Robert Burns (1759 — 1796)

'O, for my ain king,' quo' guid Wallace,
'The rightfu' king of fair Scotland,
Between me and my sovereign bluid,
I think I see ill seed sawn.'

Wallace out over yon river he lap,
And he has lighted low down on yon plain,
And he was a ware of a gay ladie,
As she was at the well washing.

'What tydins, what tydins, fair lady,' he says,
'What tydins hast thou to tell unto me;
What tydins, what tydins, fair lady,' he says,
'What tydins hae ye in the south countrie?'

'Low down in yon wee Ostler house
There is fyfteen Englishmen,
And they are seekin for guid Wallace;
It's him to take, and him to hang.'

'There's nocht in my purse,' quo' guid Wallace,
'There's nocht, not even a bare pennie;
But I will down to yon wee Ostler house
Thir fyfteen Englishmen to see.'

And when he cam in to yon wee Ostler house
He bad benedicite be there;
(The Englishmen at the table sat
The wine-fac'd captain at him did stare.)
'Where was ye born, auld crookit carl,
Where was ye born – in what countrie?'
'I am a true Scot born and bred,
And an auld crookit carl just sic as ye see.'

'I wad gie fyfteen shillings to onie crookit carl –
To onie crookit carl just sic as ye,
If ye will get me guid Wallace,
For he is the man I wad very fain see.'

He hit the proud captain alang the chaft blade
That never a bit o' meal he ate mair;
And he sticket the rest at the table where they sat,
And he left them a' lyin sprawlin there.

'Get up, get up, guidwife,' he says,
'And get to me some dinner in haste;
For it will soon be three lang days
Sin I a bit o' meat did taste.'

The dinner was na weel readie,
Nor was it on the table set,
Till other fyfteen Englishmen
Were a' lighted about the yett.

'Come out, come out, now guid Wallace,
This is the day that thou maun die.'
'I lippen nae sae little to God,' he says,
'Altho' I be but ill wordie.'

The guidwife had an auld guidman,
By guid Wallace he stiffly stood,
Till ten o' the fyfteen Englishmen
Before the door lay in their bluid.

The other five to the greenwood ran,
And he hang'd these five upon a grain;
And on the morn wi' his merry men a'
He sat at dine in Lochmaben town.

Excerpt from Verses: Written on a Foreigner's Visiting the Grave of a Swiss Gentleman, Buried among the Descendants of Sir William Wallace, Guardian of Scotland in the Thirteenth Century.

Janet Little (1759–1813)

Janet Little was an exact contemporary of Burns (both were born in 1759) and was a housemaid in the employment of Burns's patron Mrs Dunlop. This fragment about Wallace, 'The Chief,' is written in slightly stiff but eloquent English and has a marvellous final line attributed to the spirit of the hero.

Our regal seat to Edward fallen a prey,
Our Chief's insulted corse his victim lay;
Our ruin'd land no monument could raise;
Yet grateful bards still sung his heart-felt praise.
Long ages hence her hero still she'll mourn;
Still her brave sons with emulation burn.
His spirit guarding still our native place,
Proclaims this mandate to his latest race:
'Let sacred truth bid living fame be thine;
'Ne'er trust for honour to a sculptur'd shrine.
'Those modest merits marbles ne'er impart,
'Love writes them deepest on the human heart.'

On the Earl of Buchan presenting General Washington (Jan. 3 1792) with a Box, made of the Oak Tree that hid Sir William Wallace, &c.

George Galloway (unknown)

George Galloway, a Stirling burgess and radical poet pub-
lished this work in his book entitled The Tears of Poland, to
which are added songs on various subjects, Scots and English
(Edinburgh 1795). The Earl of Buchan (1742-1829) was the
first to commission a public statue of Wallace. A supporter
of the American and French Revolutions he, like Burns, viewed
Washington as a transatlantic Wallace.

Of all the heroes of antiquity,
None is more dear to fame than *Elerslie*;
Brave Hector ne'er gave Troy more relief,
Than Scotia found in her immortal chief.
Ambition led Achilles to sack Troy,
But Scotland's welfare was our hero's joy.
His country's woes, he ever mourn'd in steel,
And this blood thirsty Edward oft did feel,
When prudence taught him treach'ry to elude,
His asylum was an oak in the *Torewood*.

Hail! Nobel *Buchan*, ever prone to save,
Great Wallace memory from oblivion's cave;
So what Edinas artists rear'd to fame,
Your modest worth just compliments the fame;
To *Washington* our modern *Elerslie*,
The bane of despots, and of tyranny,
But like our *Wallace* dear to *liberty*.

Tho' glorious *Wallace* basely was betray'd,
Yet to the last he never was dismay'd;
Wishing he had more lives for to lay down,
As Martyrs for Old Scotia, and her Crown.
But vain blood-thirsty *Longshanks* soon did bleed,
When thund'ring pale destruction o'er the Tweed;
Then thought of Wallace, valour did produce
Our *freedom*, which completed was by *Bruce*.

Long may old Scotia boast a Buchan's lord,
Who stands her weal, but favour or reward;
Spurning the servile yoke of bribes and courts,
(When their infernal influence exerts,)
That we may taste of liberty a share,
The glory of our Western Hemisphere.
Since tyranny has got a mortal stab,
In each luxuriant Kingdom in the globe,
Vile despots tremble while their subjects groan,
Since *Wallace* is reviv'd in *Washington*

Lines Composed at Cora Linn, in Sight of Wallace's Tower

William Wordsworth (1770—1850)

William Wordsworth was an admirer of Burns. His various sorties to Scotland gave him much poetic inspiration, including, presumably, these lines from Book I of The Prelude, *in which the poet casts around for an appropriate subject to 'summon back from lonesome banishment,' and place 'in the hearts of men.' The beautiful waterfall on the Clyde near Lanark is traditionally associated with Wallace. An astonishing number of place names and natural features in Scotland bear Wallace's name.*

. . . I would relate
How Wallace fought for Scotland; left the name
Of 'Wallace' to be found like a wild flower
All over his dear country; left the deeds
Of Wallace, like a family of ghosts
To people the steep rocks and river banks
Her natural sanctuaries, with a local soul
Of Independence and stern Liberty.

The Death of Wallace

Robert Southey (1774–1843)

Robert Southey, Wordsworth's fellow Lake Poet, tackles the grim reality of Wallace's execution with complete sympathy for the Scottish hero. His poem emphasises the dignity retained by the stricken man in the most appalling circumstances as well as his moral superiority over the apparently triumphant Edward I. The most patriotic Scot could not look for a more positive portrayal.

    Joy, joy in London now!
He goes, the rebel Wallace goes to death,
At length the traitor meets the traitor's doom,
    Joy, joy in London now!

    He on a sledge is drawn,
His strong right arm unweapon'd and in chains,
And garlanded around his helmless head
    The laurel wreath of scorn.

    They throng to view him now
Who in the field had fled before his sword,
Who at the name of Wallace once grew pale
    And faltered out a prayer.

    Yes, they can meet his eye,
That only beams with patient courage now,
Yes, they can gaze upon those manly limbs
    Defenceless now and bound.

And that eye did not shrink
As he beheld the pomp of infamy,
Nor did one rebel feeling shake those limbs
    When the last moment came.

What though suspended sense
Was by their damned cruelty revived;
What though ingenious vengeance lengthened life
    To fell protracted death –

What though the hangman's hand
Graspt in his living breast the beating heart,
In the last agony, the last sick pang,
    Wallace had comfort still.

He called to mind his deeds
Done for his country in the embattled field;
He thought of that good cause for which he died,
    And it was joy in death!

Go, Edward, triumph now!
Cambria is fallen, and Scotland's strength is crush'd;
On Wallace, on Llewellyn's mangled limbs
    The fowls of heaven have fed.

Unrivalled, unopposed,
Go, Edward, full of glory, to thy grave!
The weight of patriot blood upon thy soul!
    Go, Edward, to thy God!

The Dirge of Wallace

Thomas Campbell (1777–1844)

Thomas Campbell ignores the tradition of the murdered Lanark wife and supposes a grieving widow in Elderslie. His poem is ingeniously crafted and in heroic language to match his theme. Indeed Wallace here takes on mythic dimensions: 'And the sword that seem'd fit for archangel to wield/ Was light in his terrible hand.'

They lighted the tapers at dead of night,
And chanted their holiest hymn,
But her brow and her bosom were damp with affright,
    Her eye was all sleepless and dim.

And the lady of Elderslie wept for her lord,
When a death-watch beat in her lonely room,
When her curtain had shook of its own accord,
And the raven had flapped at her window board,
    To tell of her warrior's doom.

Now sing the death-song and loudly pray
    For the soul of my knight so dear,
And call me a widow this wretched day,
    Since the warning of God is here.

For a nightmare rides on my strangled sleep–
The lord of my bosom is doomed to die;
His valorous heart they have wounded deep,
And the blood-red tears shall his country weep,
    For Wallace of Elderslie.

Yet knew not his country that ominous hour,
    Ere the loud matin bell was rung,
That a trumpet of death on an English tower
    Had the dirge of her champion sung.

When his dungeon light looked dim and red
On the high-born blood of a martyr slain,
No anthem was sung at his holy death-bed;
No weeping there was when his bosom bled,
    And his heart was rent in twain.

Oh! it was not thus when his oaken spear
    Was true to that knight forlorn,
And hosts of a thousand were scattered like deer
    At the sound of the hunter's horn!

When he strode o'er the wreck of each well-fought field,
    With the yellow-haired chiefs of his native land;
For his lance was not shivered on helmet or shield,
And the sword that seemed fit for archangel to wield,
    Was light in his terrible hand.

But bleeding and bound, though 'the Wallace wight,'
    For his much-lov'd country die,
The bugle ne'er sung to a braver knight
    Than Wallace of Elderslie.

But the day of his glory shall never depart,
    His head unentombed shall with glory be palmed,
From its blood-streaming altar his spirit shall start;
Though the raven has fed on his mouldering heart–
    A nobler was never embalmed.

The Lament of Wallace, After the Battle of Falkirk

(Sung to *Maids of Arrochar*)

Robert Tannahill (1774 – 1810)

The Paisley weaver-poet looks at the aftermath of the crucial lost battle through Wallace's eyes in a poem whose technical competence seems almost to detract from its tragic subject matter.

Thou dark winding Carron, once pleasing to see,
　　To me thou can'st never give pleasure again;
My brave Caledonians lie low on the lea,
　　And thy streams are deep-ting'd with the blood of the
　　　　slain.
Ah! base-hearted treachery has doom'd our undoing, –
　　My poor bleeding country, what more can I do?
Even valour looks pale o'er the red field of ruin,
　　And Freedom beholds her best warriors laid low.

Farewell, ye dear partners of peril! farewell!
　　Though buried ye lie in one wide bloody grave,
Your deeds shall ennoble the place where ye fell,
　　And your names be enroll'd with the sons of the brave.
But I, a poor outcast, in exile must wander,
　　Perhaps, like a traitor, ignobly must die!
On thy wrongs, O my country! indignant I ponder –
　　Ah! woe to the hour when thy Wallace must fly!

Address to Cartlane Craigs

John Jamieson, DD (1759—1838)

*This nineteenth-century poem is by a Scots divine and scholar
whose conventional, flowery language can't altogether obscure
substance and originality, from the opening conceit that free-
dom can be found like a fossil or a plant in the Lanarkshire
landscape so closely associated with the Wallace ('Him – who
could not be taught to crouch').*

Ye Cartlane Craigs, your steepy sides
    Let Nature's votaries explore,
To learn what fossils here she hides,
    Or find some plant unknown before.

A far more precious vein I seek;
    And here, I know, 'twas once conceal'd;
A simple – that can nerve the weak,
    And prowess to the fearful yield.

Blest Freedom flourish'd in this wild,
    When banish'd from each cultur'd spot:
Expiring Albin saw, and smil'd,
    And all her wounds and woes forgot.

And still the rugged rock, fair plant,
    'Hath been thy lov'd, thy native soil;
Remote from Luxury's deadly haunt,
    Thy dwelling 'mongst the sons of toil.

Thy arms entwin'd around the rock,
    And shrouded by a fleece of snow,
The tyrant-tempest thou canst mock,
    That rudely strives to lay thee low.

Ye towering cliffs, your form upright,
    The awful frown ye downward send,
Seem to portray that faithful knight,
    Who to his foes would never bend.

I love thy' gloom, thou cavern drear;
    Such magic influence quite unfelt,
Where lordly domes their turrets rear;
    – Here Freedom and her First-born dwelt.

Hence bursting, like the wrathful blast,
    That issues from thy hollow glade,
To hostile Lanark Wallace pass'd,
    And low the haughty *Southeron* laid.

But why a pledge so precious left?
    Thou, Chieftain, might'st thy foes have known
– Of life thy lovely partner's reft,
    Of life – far dearer than thy own.

Base *Hesilrig*, I hate thy name!
    Thy crime a Pompey's praise would mar;
A woman slay! – thou soldier's shame!
    With women only coulds't thou war.

Yet worthy thou of such a lord;
    And school'd his purpose to fulfil,
No right who knowledg'd, but the sword,
    No reason, save his sovereign will:

The forms of justice, if employ'd,
    Who still her sacred essence scorn'd;
Each faithful witness first destroy'd,
    Then Falsehood's base-born brood suborn'd.

An ancient kingdom, could he think,
    The scourge of his, – might thus be won?
Thy name, crown'd traitor, still shall stink,
    While Albin boasts one freeborn son!

Thou, Edward, many a traitor vile,
    – Thy kindred true – didst aggrandize:
Nor force, nor flattery, – dastard guile
    Alone, could Wallace make thy prize.

Him – who could not be taught to crouch,
    Nor grace, nor justice, thine to save:
Thou knew'st our Lion ne'er would couch,
    While Wallace liv'd his keeper brave.

His name, who Scotia's fetters broke,
    Shall never lose its power to charm,
Who liv'd to shield her, – dying spoke
    The weakness of her spoiler's arm.

The Battle of Stirling

William Sinclair (1811–unknown)

*Another mid-nineteenth century poem, this time a vigorous
retelling of the Battle of Stirling Bridge. The rather odd last
verse ('Thy pulse, O Freedom! still shall beat/ With the throb
of manhood's prime!') has a pious imperial invocation of sham-
rock and rose as well as thistle.*

To Scotland's ancient realm
Proud Edward's armies came,
To sap our freedom, and o'erwhelm
    Our martial force in shame:
'It shall not be!' brave Wallace cried;
'It shall not be!' his chiefs replied;
    'By the name our fathers gave her,
Our steel shall drink the crimson stream,
We'll all her dearest rights redeem–
    Our own broadswords shall save her!'

With hopes of triumph flush'd,
    The squadrons hurried o'er
Thy bridge, Kildean, and heaving rush'd
    Like wild waves to the shore
'They come – they come!' was the gallant cry;
'They come – they come!' was the loud reply;
    'O strength, though gracious Giver!
By Love and Freedom's stainless faith,
We'll dare the darkest night of death–
    We'll drive them back for ever!'

All o'er the waving broom,
 In chivalry and grace,
Shone England's radiant spear and plume,
 By Stirling's rocky base:
And, stretching far beneath the view,
Proud Cressingham! thy banners flew,
 When, like a torrent rushing,
O God! From right and left the flame
Of Scottish swords like lightning came,
 Great Edward's legions crushing!

High praise, ye gallant band,
 Who, in the face of day,
With a daring heart and a fearless hand,
 Have cast your chains away!
The foemen fell on every side–
In crimson hues the Forth was dyed–
 Bedew'd with blood the heather,
While cries triumphal shook the air–
'Thus shall they do, thus shall they dare,
 Wherever Scotsmen gather!'

Though years like shadows fleet
 O'er the dial-stone of Time,
Thy pulse, O Freedom! still shall beat
 With the throb of manhood's prime!
Still shall the valour, love, and truth,
That shone on Scotland's early youth,
 From Scotland ne'er dissever;
The Shamrock, Rose, and Thistle stern
Shall wave around her Wallace cairn
 And bless the brave for ever!

Verses on Wallace's Cave in Cadzow Forest

Andrew Hamilton (unknown–1898)

A tribute to one of the many Scottish locations and natural features associated with the hero.

'Wallace trees in the woods, Wallace caves in the glens,
Wallace-seats on the hills. Wallace stones on the plains.
On the face of the country is graven his fame,
For tradition links all with the patriot's name.'

Though rough and rugged be this place,
    Let Scotsmen love it and revere,
For from his cruel 'Southron faes'   English foes, or enemies
    The Wallace found a refuge here.

These ancient towering rocks around,
    Once echoed to the hero's tread;
This gloomy cavern's hoary bounds
    Once sheltered his devoted head.

That linn his lullaby once sung,
    When couched upon a rocky bed,
This Royal Oak once o'er him flung
    Its leafy screen and verdant shade.

The patriot here to Heaven vowed
    To liberate his father-land
From grasp of England's despot proud,
    And 'beard to beard' meet with his band.

Oh sure the place must worthy be
    Of veneration and esteem,
That sheltered such a one as he,

    Our nation's glory, and her shame.
And cold his heart as is the steel –
    As Scotsman I deny his claim –
That does not thrill of rapture feel
    In such a place at such a name.

Not princely halls of regal state,
    Where wreaths are hung and trophies wave,
Such deep impressions can create
    As can Sir William Wallace cave.

Author's Note:

This cave is situated in the High Parks of Hamilton. A tradition current in the neighbourhood associates it with the immortal Wallace. That 'great patriot-hero ill-requitted chief.' Though rather difficult to access and exit, it is well worthy a visit from every lover of the picturesque; for, independently of its tradionary [sic] association with the 'Hero of Scotland', it is romantic in the highest degree. Such places ought to be held in everlasting remembrance by all Scotsmen, for in them the war-councils of Wallace and his companions were held, which eventually led to the deliverance of Scotland from 'Edward, chains and slaverie.' – A.H.

A Summary History of Sir William Wallace

William McGonagall (1825 – 1902)

*The unique talent of Dundee's own ineffable poet and trage-
dian William McGonagall is brought to bear on the Wallace
story. Two early fatal encounters with Englishmen form the
bulk of the text. There are some vintage couplets. The hero is
thereafter dispatched rather perfunctorily.*

Sir William Wallace of Ellerslie,
I'm told he went to the High School in Dundee,
For to learn to read and write,
And after that he learned to fight.
While at the High School in Dundee,
The Provost's son with him did disagree,
Because Wallace he did wear a dirk,
He despised him like an ignorant stirk,
Which with indignation he keenly felt,
And told him it would become him better in his belt.

Then Wallace's blood began to boil,
Just like the serpent in its coil,
Before it leaps upon its prey;
And unto him he thus did say:
'Proud, saucy cur, come cease your prate,
For no longer I shall wait,
For to hear you insult me,
At the High School in Dundee;
For such insolence makes my heart to smart,
And I'll plunge my dagger in your heart.'

Portrait of Wallace painted 1660 for Niddrie Marischal House, Edinburgh, and enlarged with a martial trophy in the 1720s. The second oldest extant portrait of Wallace.
Stirling Smith Art Gallery and Museum.

Portrait of Wallace, 17th century, now in Torosay Castle, Isle of Mull.
Stirling Smith Art Gallery and Museum / SCRAN.

Portrait of Wallace, c1740 by William Robertson.
Stirling Smith Art Gallery and Museum.

Wallace chapbook, Glasgow, c1800. The printer has used an engraving which is more commonly found on chapbooks about Bruce and other monarchs.
Stirling Smith Art Gallery and Museum.

Face of the colossal statue at Dryburgh commissioned by David Steuart Erskine, Earl of Buchan in 1814. Sculpted by John Smith of Darnick.
Stirling Smith Art Gallery and Museum.

Nineteenth-century portrait of William Wallace using the iconography of the dragon-helmeted and bearded warrior favoured by the Earl of Buchan.

Stirling Smith Art Gallery and Museum.

SIR WILLIAM WALLACE
From Elderslie to Robroyston.

By Rev. J. F. Miller, M.A., Millerston.

IN HONOUR OF
WILLIAM WALLACE
GUARDIAN OF SCOTLAND

WALLACE MONUMENT, ABERDEEN.

Wallace statue, Aberdeen by William Grant Stevenson (1849-1919), unveiled 29 June 1888. This is the finest of the Wallace statues. Recently restored, it is the focus of an annual pageant and ceremony celebrating Wallace's place in Scottish history.

Stirling Smith Art Gallery and Museum.

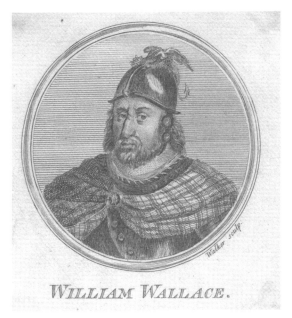

WILLIAM WALLACE.

Jug with a crude but recognisable Wallace portrait.
Probably Scottish, 1870-1900.
Stirling Smith Art Gallery and Museum.

Tokens, 1797, showing Scotland Resurgent on the obverse and Wallace on the reverse. These were commissioned by Colonel William Fullerton, but were banned on account of being too close to coin of the Realm, by a government nervous of the revolutions in France and America.

Stirling Smith Art Gallery and Museum/Private Collection.

Watercolour by Andrew Munro, Bard of the Clan MacDonald, used as a preface to a manuscript copy of his Wallace poem, 1908. The group of houses are those at Elderslie, Paisley, thought to be the birthplace of Wallace, which were demolished by the local authority in the 1970s.

Stirling Smith Art Gallery and Museum.

Wallace statue, Ballarat, Melbourne, Australia, bequeathed by Scottish patriot James Russell Thomson. Sculpted by Percival Ball of Melbourne, who used Scottish athlete Donald Dinnie (1837-1916), the finest example of Scottish manhood available, for his model; unveiled 1889.

Stirling Smith Art Gallery and Museum.

Victorian scrap of Wallace, c1870, one of a series on famous Scots.

Stirling Smith Art Gallery and Museum.

Scottish archer in Wallace's army, by Andrew Munro, New York, 1908.

Stirling Smith Art Gallery and Museum.

Equestrian portrait of Wallace by Andrew Munro, New York, 1908.

Stirling Smith Art Gallery and Museum.

Top left: Lord Lamington and his sister Marion Braidfute, wife of William Wallace, by Andrew Munro, New York, 1908.

Top right: The Earl of Douglas by Andrew Munro, New York, 1908.

Bottom right: A Scottish soldier in Wallace's Army by Andrew Munro, New York, 1908.

Stirling Smith Art Gallery and Museum.

A grander man ne'er trod.

Page 91.

Portrait of Wallace by Andrew Munro, New York, 1908.

Stirling Smith Art Gallery and Museum.

Statue of Wallace at Dryburgh, the first public work to be commissioned. The statue's height is 21½ feet, and the piece including the plinth is 30 feet. Sculpted by John Smith of Darnick; unveiled 1814.

Stirling Smith Art Gallery and Museum.

WALLACE STATUE
St BOSWELLS

Statue of Wallace by Robert Forrest (1789-1852) on St Nicholas' Church, Lanark, 1821. The statue is a focus of the Lanimer Day celebrations in the town.

Stirling Smith Art Gallery and Museum.

Statue in "ye Old Tolbooth," Newmarket St., Ayr.

Statue in Newmarket Street, Ayr, 1819. The sculptor is believed to be William Reid of Ayr who carved a marble bust of Wallace in 1802 for Frances Wallace Dunlop, a friend of the poet Burns.

Stirling Smith Art Gallery and Museum.

'The Wee Wallace' by Alexander Handyside Ritchie (1804-1870), Corn Exchange, Stirling, 1859. Ritchie's work was commissioned by William Drummond (1793-1868), Seed Merchant, and the statue's title distinguishes it from the large Wallace statue by D. W. Stevenson (1887) on the National Wallace Monument.

Stirling Smith Art Gallery and Museum.

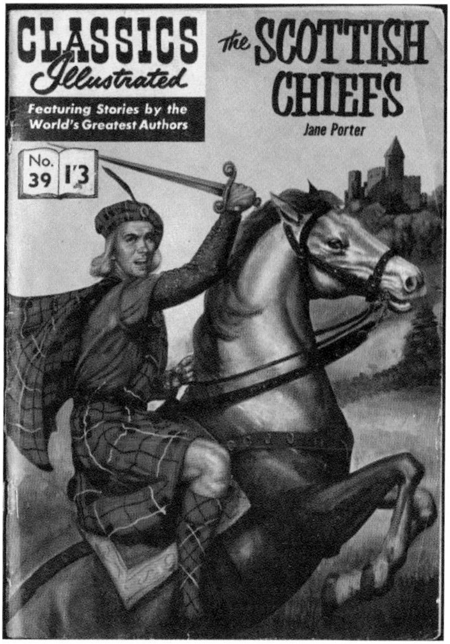

The Scottish Chiefs by Jane Porter (1810); 1950s Classics Illustrated Edition, with Wallace on the cover.

Stirling Smith Art Gallery and Museum.

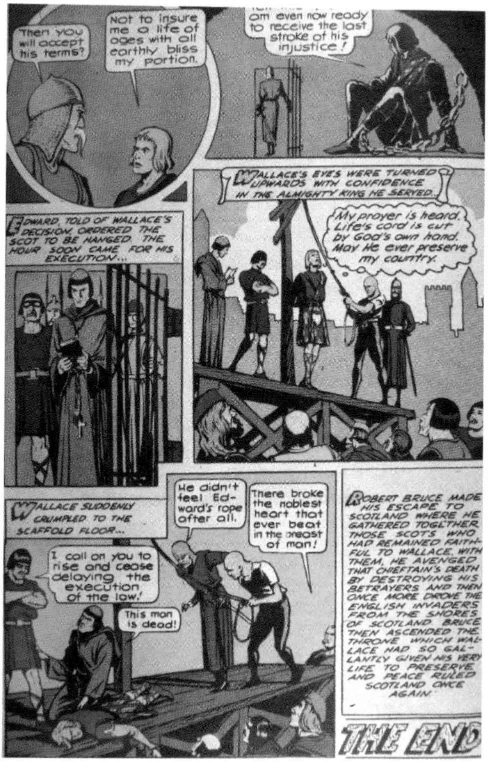

The death of Wallace from *The Scottish Chiefs*, 1950s Classics Illustrated Edition.

Stirling Smith Art Gallery and Museum.

John Blair, monk of Dunfermline, presents his *Life of Wallace* to
Bishop Sinclair of Dunkeld who

Himself he had seen the most of Wallace's deeds
His purpose was to have it sent to Rome
Our Father of Kirk theron to give his doom

Linocut by Owain Kirby 1997.
Stirling Smith Art Gallery and Museum.

The vision of Wallace in Monkton Kirk, Ayr. According to Blind Harry,
Wallace had a vision of Scotland on fire from Ross to the Solway. An old
man (St Andrew) presented him with a sword with which to free Scotland.
A beautiful woman (the Blessed Virgin) gave him the rods of governance.
Linocut by Owain Kirby, 1997.

Stirling Smith Art Gallery and Museum.

Blind Harry sings the songs of Wallace at the Court of James IV. Linocut by Owain Kirby, 1997.

Stirling Smith Art Gallery and Museum.

Quilt commemorating David R. Ross's Walk for Wallace made by Armadale Primary School Primary 7 Class 2003–2004 and teacher Audra McKee.

Stirling Smith Art Gallery and Museum.

Then his heart's blood did quickly flow,
And poor Wallace did not know where to go;
And he stood by him until dead.
Then far from him he quickly fled,
Lamenting greatly the deed he had done,
The murdering of the Provost's son.

The scene shifts to where he was fishing one day,
Where three English soldiers met him by the way,
And they asked him to give them some fish,
And from them they would make a delicious dish.
Then Wallace gave them share of his fish,
For to satisfy their wish;
But they seemed dissatisfied with the share they got,
So they were resolved to have all the lot.

Then Wallace he thought it was time to look out,
When they were resolved to have all his trout;
So he swung his fishing-rod with great force round his
    head,
And struck one of them a blow that killed him dead;
So he instantly seized the fallen man's sword,
And the other two fled without uttering a word.

Sir William Wallace of Ellerslie,
You were a warrior of great renown,
And might have worn Scotland's crown;
Had it not been for Monteith, the base traitor knave,
That brought you to a premature grave;
Yes! you were sold for English gold,
And brought like a sheep from the fold,
To die upon a shameful scaffold high,
Amidst the derisive shouts of your enemies standing by.

But you met your doom like a warrior bold,
Bidding defiance to them that had you sold,
And bared your neck for the headsman's stroke;
And cried, 'Marion, dear, my heart is broke;
My lovely dear, I come to thee,
Oh! I am longing thee to see!'
But the headsman was as stolid as the rock,
And the axe fell heavily on the block,
And the scaffold did shake with the terrible shock,
As the body of noble Wallace fell,
Who had fought for Scotland so well.

William Wallace
for the Ballarat Statue of Him

Francis Lauderdale Adams (1862–1893)

These lines are carved on the Wallace statue in Ballarat,
Victoria, Australia, showing that the reputation of Wallace
had been taken across the globe by Scottish immigrants to
Australia more than a century ago.

This is Scotch William Wallace. It was he
Who in dark hours first raised his face to see:
Who watched the English tyrant nobles spurn,
Steel-clad, with iron hoofs the Scottish free:

Who armed and drilled the simple footman Kern,
Yea, bade in blood and rout the proud knight learn
His feudalism was dead, and Scotland stand
Dauntless to wait the day of Bannockburn.

O Wallace, peerless lover of thy land
We need thee still, thy moulding brain and hand.
For us, thy poor, again proud tyrants spurn,
The robber rich, a yet more hateful band.

Part Two

Modern poems, stage and radio interpretations inspired by Wallace

This section of the book collects contemporary responses to William Wallace and his story. Many of the poems were written specifically for the collection. They run in alphabetical order of authors.

William Wallace at Westminster, 1305

James S. Adam

James S. Adam was inspired by lines carved on the base of the Wallace statue in Aberdeen: 'To Edward King of England I cannot be a traitor. He is not my sovereign. I owe him no allegiance. He has never received homage from me and while life is in this persecuted body, he never shall receive it.' Adam comments: 'Graund tho the leid is, we can be shair that Wallys wadna hae uised modern English speak, sae here it is in modern Scots at sets his thochts better. I hae uised a makar's freedom tae bring in ither sayins linkit wi Wallys an his fecht for his ain kintra an his ain fowk, sayins at onie an every Scot och tae hae in his hairt an mynd the day, the morn, an for aye.

Tae Edward o England nae traitors are we.
Aa Scots share ae gift wha were born tae byde free;
Our kings we aye wale by a richt we'll ne'er tyne
an bi that same richt ye are nae king o mine;
there's nane o your race that can lay claim on me
while our bluid proclaims we'll hae nae slaverie;
proud Edward, ye've ne'er seen ma knee tae ye bend;
an ne'er will you see it tho ma corp ye may rend;
the Scot wha ne'er crouched tae the Roman lang syne
will cour in nae bondage tae your lesser line;
a priest I revered tellt me man's greatest gift
was aye tae walk free neath the licht o God's lift;
that freedom that rings thru our lang historie,
I shairly will threip in the daith I maun dee.

Tae makk a Martyr

Sheena Blackhall

Aberdeen-based Blackhall has published more than 40 books of poetry and writes both in English and Doric. A former fellow of the Elphinstone Institute, Aberdeen University, she is engaged in fostering creative writing, particularly in the vernacular.

Takk ae patriot
Separate him frae kintra, kin an airmy
Croon him wi leaves like ony tattie-bogle
Makk a radge o him an his beliefs

Add nae drap o human kindness, raither
A scoosh o soor grapes, wersh as graveyaird bree
Sprinkle a jeelip o heich wirds ower the proceedins

Wheep yer warrior, bleedin ben the streets
Larded wi gobs an skaith
Beat till nearhaun fooshionless
Afore a fyauchie boorich o yer commons
Hing on the gallows till hauf-smored an thrappled

Neist, remove yer patriot,
Skewer an disembowel
While yet alive . . . hate is a dish best hett

Fry his intimmers aneth his verra een
Syne chop the lave an sen tae aa the airts
Sae his puir pairts micht flegg aff similar craas
Nailin oppression's colours tae life's brig

Sit back an wyte
There's mair nur deid-flesh stewin

Author's Note:

The Wallace Statue in Aberdeen, erected in 1888, bears this
inscription reputed to have been uttered to the patriot by his
uncle: 'I tell you a truth, liberty is the best of all things my
son, never live under any slavish bond'. Local legend con-
tends that the portion of the dismembered Wallace received
by the city is built into the wall of St Machar's Cathedral,
the spot being marked by a star shape.

There's no memorial at Stirling Bridge

Christopher Brookes

This poem was written by an English visitor to Stirling after seeing the movie Braveheart, *and was first printed in the* Stirling Observer.

There's no memorial at Stirling Bridge
just a communal field, tight-pinioned, emasculate
by council housing, arterial road and underpass.
But one bare patch of eloquence:
old spreading tree sheltering littered bench
by the dark turbidity of the Forth.
There, where endless eddies of abandoned fizz-can
echo Scotland's age-old fates
and the gaunt bridge, bearing ancient arch
itself replacement for time-lost wooden span
where Wallace and his Scotland's pride
fought that long-gone bloodied, barbed day.
Stirling survives; its pageantry now tourist tide
built round bobbing Bruce and his Bannockburned day
and the doomed Stewart line.
Yet this field is Braveheart's yet
his own, crowned monument on Abbey Craig, still shouts
coherent, full defined:
defiance of London's tyranny enthroned
urges Scots ahead, to greater days!

Wha Hae

Angus Calder

*Edinburgh-based Angus Calder is an historian, academic, jour-
nalist and literary commentator, as well as a poet. His spare
poem leaves much open to imagination and interpretation.*

Where do the people march –

east

    south
        west?

What is this gap in the air –

rock
    pinetree

        eagle?

What is this voice in the wind –

ballad

    pibroch

        battlecry?

What man with no face leads the march –

swordsman
      vagabond
            prophet?

Skull of whom set on that pole?

We believe it was Wallace.

Receiving a Traitor's Leg, Perth, 1305

Fergus Chadwick

A grisly reminder of the actual aftermath of Wallace's execution, the poem projects quite powerfully into the mind of the contemporary observer.

Quarters received at Perth;
Newcastle, Stirling, Berwick. . .
Not my job to say this isn't
a quarter, only a naked leg
with some buttock pertaining.
Think of the way it's come
(or rather don't); the hessian
sack loosely tied, studded
with flies; labelled 'Wallace,
one quarter to Perth', et cetera.
Dogs must've eaten the toes.
What a stink, lolloping
to and fro in a red cart. . .
Hammer it onto the spike,
then; stand back; a rich sight.
Pearly maggots escaping
drip from the hero's wounds.
Run, crook leg, run away now
If you can, poor bastard, Wallace.
Nowhere now to cross your legs
under oaken tables of state,

your foot-pulse twitching damask.
Dancing flies, and many wings
fan a black wafting stench. . .
Why me that always gets this job?
Noboby owns this rotting leg.
Mine, the last hand, runs up it
slowly in a sighing stroke.
Where its twin is, God knows;
Stirling probably, day's travel
in between the fork girls eyed.
His legs then spun a reel,
a full calf flexing proud and white;
stockinged feet landing no more
than an instant on fire-lit boards
that jumped with whooping rhythm!
Is this a man? Is this like mine?
My legs move, one after the other
downwards, round the spiral stairs.

Ballad For Sir William Wallace

Lady Isobel Wren, aka Sarah Dorrance-Minch

This is a modern poem about Wallace but in traditional form. The author explains: 'Technically this isn't a ballade at all, but something called a chaunt royale, a very late period form introduced to the English by Chaucer but not used frequently until the time of John Donne.'

A cruel day it was, in that seventh month,
When the English monarch cross'd the Tweed,
Hot with wrath at the Scottish affront,
Heart set to avenge a humiliating deed.
But ten months past, his troops met defeat.
But ten months past, 'twas Cressingham's conceit
That saw the English scatter'd and slain.
The Scots thought to free themselves of his reign,
Heedless to loss or great sacrifice –
They knew full well, though it were writ in pain,
Life is dear, but freedom without price.
'Twas in September they sought to confront
the English troops, their advance to impede;
No machines of war, but only blunt
pikes of wood had they; but concede
they did not. Nay, e'en out number'd, in the heat
of battle they yet went forth, the enemy to greet.
On the muddy field, the blood fell as rain.
They trapped the tyrant's host on that plain

by desperate courage and cunning device.
On Scotland, the glory; on England, the stain.
Life is dear, but freedom without price.
Was it to Surrey naught but a hunt?
Or was it tight-purs'd Cressingham's greed?
Ay they laugh'd at the 'poor peasant stunt'
and plann'd their ride homeward with all Godspeed –
An easy victory in their hands. Sweet
was the gain they tasted. But incomplete
were their plans; they thought to cross the Forth in vain.
No ford was there. Two rivers, and between
them but a swan's neck of land. In a trice
The Scottish host swarm'd down. The English were slain.
Life is dear, but freedom without price.
And thus it chanc'd the Plantagenet to confront
Brave Wallace; full of only one need,
That to devour him. At Falkirk the front
of English host made the land bleed –
To the great horde, the rebels were but meat
To their blades. Their leader knew defeat:
'Dance if you can,' said he, in his eyes plain
The slaughter. Death was before them, but no chain
Would they wear. For them only the prize,
whether death or vict'ry, was meet –
Life was dear, but freedom without price.
The archers fell forward. With a grunt
The rebel pikemen fell, and the Tweed
ran red with blood. Beneath the affront
The Scots forces shatter'd. The field cried
with the moans of the dead. Victory complete,

the Scots betrayed, the English savour'd their sweet
success. They ground their brethren beneath them again,
And Edward grew fat and secure in his reign,
Ne'er thinking that one might him unseat.
Life is dear, and freedom without price.

L'ENVOI

At Bannockburn, seventeen years hence, the English met
    defeat,
The Scots drank revenge, and the taste was sweet,
Though costlier than the rarest spice.
Three hundred years pass'd e'er Scone the Lion met.
Life is dear, but freedom without price.

A Towering Presence

Lesley Duncan

The National Wallace Monument, Stirling, built by public subscription in the 1860s, occupies a commanding position above the River Forth and is the grandest of the towers raised to the hero in the nineteenth century.

How *did* the architect Rochead conceive
This monument, at once magnificent and
Slightly monstrous (like the patriot himself),
With asymmetric lines that disconcert?
Victorian gothic, yes; but more than that,
As if the spirit of the butchered Wallace,
Disdaining braveheart brigadooneries,
Was embodied with his massive sword
Within the soaring stonework, itself a
Potent emblem of the emasculated hero;
While through the carse below,
The river coils like silver entrails in the sun,
Where Stirling Bridge was won.

This building provokes simile and metaphor.
See it poised for lift-off against the backdrop
Of the Ochil Hills in whin or heather time,
Theatrically unreal against the stippled scenery.
In heavy autumn mist it disappears,
An absent presence on the Abbey Craig,
Or sometimes juts above the clouds,
A rocket-head poised heavenwards.

I've seen it haloed by a rainbow.
Its many faces seem to symbolise
The complex man himself in varied guise.

In winter dark the floodlit tower
Confronts the castle on its rock.
The two swap semaphores across the plain
Of old heroic deeds, triumph and pain.

Scotland's Shame

Brian D. Finch

Brian D. Finch's poetry, as shown in his collection Talking with Tongues *(Luath Press, 2003), ranges in theme from the Dark Ages to Desert Storm and the Dunblane massacre. His engagement simultaneously with history and contemporary issues is demonstrated in this poem.*

I neither mourn the late Black Watch
nor yet the Royal Scots
nor King's Own Scottish Borderers
nor weep for other clots

that wandered east and south and north
enslaving black and brown
and pillaged half the world's wealth
to deck the English crown

with Koh-i-Noor and Cullinan
and Elgin's stolen stones
while guarding poppy-pushing hongs
that junkie millions cloned

as Alba's glens and straths were cleared
and weeping bairns made space
for stag and grouse and black-faced yowes
and deserts life displaced.

But I shall sing of Robert Burns
heap praise on John Maclean
and Thomas Muir of Huntershill
who saw, to Scotland's shame,

that some who prate of liberty
and damn opression's pains
are bought and sold for English gold
and dare not slip their chains.

And chief of those I celebrate
great Wallace will I sing
and free-born Scots who live unbought
and own no English king.

Guardian Gargantuan

Alistair Findlay

*Alistair Findlay's survey of Wallace's life has a certain grim wit,
from the word play of the first four lines to the final tilting at
Mel Gibson, who portrayed Wallace in the film* Braveheart *in
spite of being a much smaller man than records show Wallace
to have been.*

He gave no quarter,
or so they said,
to monk or nun,
and so they quartered him,
spiked his head on London Bridge,
and sent his left leg to Aberdeen.
Course, he was no saint –
made a belt for his sword from what
was left of Cressingham's skin,
(a rogue who fell at Stirling Bridge)
but then, he'd no more use for it.

This is how it was,
the medieval gargoyle scene.
It said: low-borns don't rebel
against suzerain – slavery
to you and me – the kind
Imperial Rome and Viking
offered Pict and Celt until
the Irish Scots redd them up
thro' centuries of struggle,

and then the schiltroms – rows of
Scottish pikes, formed in squares,
who stood, and took the full
brunt of horse and knight
and didn't break or run,
then banjoed all to Hell.

So, they spiked his head,
but they forgot about his tongue,
not the Latin or the French of course,
but the leid, the speak the Commons spoke,
the Inglis of Chaucer and Fordun, that told
the tale Blind Harry told from the telling of
the folk down thro' centuries of myth,
imagination and craving.

And as for the man himself, well,
we know he stood six and a half feet,
we have his sword at Stirling still,
two foot taller than Mel Gibson,
and Mel standing on a horse.

Excerpt from **Whaur's Yer Willie Wallace Noo?**

John Fowler

A quiet moment from John Fowler's 1976 play, reflecting the episode in Blind Harry when Wallace, after escaping from his English captors in Ayr, is saved from death and nourished by a woman. Women, in addition to the Lanark wife or sweetheart, have a contributory role in the story of Wallace. Even Edward I's Queen is shown negotiating with, and possibly lusting after, Wallace in Blind Harry.

BLIND HARRY

Nursed by the mother
And nourished by the girl
He hit under the attic thatch
Hoarding spent strength like a miser
And nobody knew he was there

English hobnails clattered on the cobbles
And shadows passed across the window
The rent man called

But nobody say the man in a dark corner
Skin stretched like oilcloth over bone
And mighty muscle shrunken in
A shadow in the armchair by the fire
When nights were cold.

Barnweil Hill, by Craigie

Gordon Jarvie

The poet visits the vantage point from where Wallace is sup-
posed to have watched a grim episode from Blind Harry,
when his fighters took terrible revenge on the English garrison
in Ayr after a massacre of Scots. The Wallace Tower at Barn-
weil, erected in the nineteenth century, is a prominent feature
of the Ayrshire landscape.

Then: 1296

Distant defiance of blue Arran hill,
white mirror slash of water in the sun,
an airy sky goes whistling by,
the Barns o Ayr burn weel, quo I,
where Braveheart went in for the kill.

There fell the English governor of Ayr
with his lippy bumptious myrmidons.
The patriot Wallace dished out justice there
and even the town's friar deaf to their orisons –
for hadn't they just tricked and slaughtered Scotia's sons?

Now: 1996

Today four of us sit in the car
by a whitewashed hilltop farm
and a tree-girt sandstone monument:
two old ladies enjoy the summer view,

a boy itches to explore it all, and I.
A lazy dog in the farmyard barks,
the blue sky fills with the singing of larks,
life tiptoes by.

A notice regrets the Wallace Tower is shut,
but the farmer has slung a long rope swing
from a high-branched elm nearby. So,
good as it might have been to climb that stair,
the boy from the car wastes little time to show
a better way up through the lark-filled air
to celebrate the deeds of Braveheart, the hero.

Braveheart!

David Kinloch

David Kinloch takes a satirical look at Mel Gibson and his portrayal of Wallace in Braveheart. *To compound the literary joke he does so in the persona of the nineteenth-century American poet Walt Whitman. Clever stuff.*

Preceded by his manager, he surges out of the dim interior of the hotel, light-footed, graceful, a clear far-away look in his eyes...

Comment faire le Tour

O Mel! Mel of the hair extenders! Braveheart!
O Mad Mac Mel! It is I,
Walt, Walt Whitman, who salutes you.
When I heard at the close of the day
That your heroic film of the Wallace
Would premiere in Stirling, I floated

From Mount Florida, high above Glasgow, floated
From the residence of my comrade Kinloch, a brave heart
Like you, I crossed the hummock-land of Shotts as Wallace
Did on leaving Elderslie, I
Sped through that dun-coloured upland (beside the great
    M8) that day
To celebrate your epic but most of all to be with you

O Mel! But also to petition you,
Dark singer of Democracy, you who floated
Like a Moses through Scottish bogs, waiting for the day
To release your noble, simple people, their brave brave
    heart
Clasped in an English vice. O Mel, I
Confuse you, mix you in my mind with Wallace.

And who could blame me? For you and Wallace
Commingle in my scented breast, you
Two and I, comrades all, shooting the film of liberty I
Crave about all else, I crave and lost as my successors
    floated
Back up stream to a land of villanelles and sonnets.
    Bravehearts!
Brave Walt! a bearded Ariel imprisoned in a bad sestina
    who would
this day

Be free again by your example, free today
To live today, to sing the love of comrades as Wallace
Did. He could not rhyme, his only beat the braveheart
Quad-pumping the eclectic plaid about his knees (What
    knees!). You
Saw him Mel, as clearly as I see you who floated
From Australia via Hollywood to this premiere. I

Name the perfumed guests as they arrive, I
Shake the manly hand of Jodie Foster, day
Dream as Christian Slater – he of the slow doe-eyes –
    floats
In. We sit transfixed as the credits of your Wallace
Roll but I have eyes alone for you,
Peach of a biceps – your musk white thighs – muncher of
                        power breakfasts, Braveheart!

Mel Wallace, Will Gibson, this day
Your barbaric yawp injects its braveheart
Into me. You and I floating and free.

The Guairdian Wallace

T.S. Law (1916–1997)

In uncompromising Scots, T.S. Law shows Wallace in chains
but equally uncompromisingly defiant towards Edward I.
The second, short, poem lists his qualities.

The Guairdian Wallace lies in chains,
An glowerin in his face,
King Edwart sees whit free men see,
King Edwart's ain disgrace.
'Weel may ye stert an turn awo
that hated Wallace free;
I never was yer vassal man,
I'd shuinner thole tae dee.'

'For lang, lang years the drookit seas
rowed soor an saut as sin,
the-tyme the rain bi shuch an burn
garred monie the reevir rin:
and ootwith Hell or inwith Hell
thae years thur dooble span,
it's I wuid byde, an better byde,
nor be King Edwart's man'

'Oor paer folk waarsle wi the grund,
an plowter shuch tae shuch;
they struissle wi the wuins an weet,
but that's clean wark enyuch.
I'd raither be a docken leaf
thur thyucks tae chack it thru,
nor be King Edwart's vassal man
an gurrie lyke a soo.'

'Then hing an draw and quarter me,
an sned me o ma heid,
an ryve the flesh fae aff ma baens
tae please yer buhllduag breed.
I haenae seen the differ yit,
disprove it gif ye can,
atween duag-beast an knicht-at-airms
whan he's King Edwart's man.'

Author's Note:

The tune I yaissed for the sang abuin is cad *Breacan Mairi
Uisdean*, haein heard it played bi a pype baun at Elderslie
no that lang afore 20 August 1967, the day I made the sang.
Later, in 11 August 1977, I puit the sang in prent in *A Pryle
o Aces*.

The Martyr

T.S. Law (1916–1997)

Anger and airmit fecht, an syne the daith
or freedom's greinin bears the gree for men.
Guid Wallace guairdian, martyr, brocht tae weire
mair nor the buskin o his fechtin gear,
a hert mair stoore nor steel amang his graith,
a siccar mynd straucht as the fedderit flane
that flichtit Stirlin Brig whaur Scotland saw
the padayne o his anger's wapinschaw.

Empire is cauld-steel skaith, a thing ootwith
soothfast ingyne an skowth stravaigin braid
or Smithfield slauchter maks the man a myth
ootbydein empire an the hero's trade:
but faith, steadfastness, siccar Wallace brocht;
dae we gie Scotland aa the martyr socht?

The Fabled Field

Maurice Lindsay

Maurice Lindsay, the veteran poet, editor, broadcaster, and television executive, recalls a distant outdoor meeting in Selkirk where he shared a platform with Wendy Wood, the celebrated nationalist; and ponders, in the modern world, the nature of national identity and Scottishness and the debt to Wallace and Bruce.

In the heat of a sunny July Selkirk day
a betartaned patriot ranted of Wallace and Bruce,
a sort of incantation merely to say
their names aloud, flaunting the unioned truce
that out of fractured centuries had been paid
to end the hostility of ancient division,
while I waited my patient turn through this verbal cascade
to talk about unifying television.
However naively out-of-date I thought
such raw-edged nationalism, the fact remains
Wallace, against the odds, once gallantly fought
the English, clearing the way for Bruce's gains
that shaped our sense of nationhood, enduring
in privacy and silently reassuring.

Forty or fifty years, I guess, must have passed
since that burnished afternoon, when a local crowd
decked out in scarce-worn summer finery, massed
to hear a feisty lady utter aloud
a normally apprehended sentiment;

while the TV fellow waited, without whose report
on the box that night their day would not have been lent
its full significance, selling them somehow short.
News every minute, some a resolved suppose,
most of it never becoming history,
substancing how we live, though it rarely shows,
unless it be tragic or unsolved mystery.
Yet that trivial afternoon so long gone by
still flashes across the screen of my inner eye;

The bright-lit images of it that survive
are that tight-knit little crowd, grey Border stone;
the corporate sense, each one of us alone
with our vacant thoughts or unacknowledged doubts
that the raised-up shrill of spontaneous protest flouts
however strong the conviction by which it is led:
though backgrounding our indefinable pride
in Scottishness, still leaves us clearly able
to see humanity thus dignified,
the symbols of each once-victorious field
mere icons on imagination's shield.

Song of Wallace

Rowena M. Love

Ayrshire-based Rowena M. Love uses a sustained musical metaphor for her consideration of Wallace's life and legacy.

'I have brought you to the ring, now see if you can dance' – Wallace's words to his army before the Battle of Falkirk

In the discord of distant days,
seven hundred years ago,
came this hero
on a legendary scale,
his huge sword a baton
conducting men in pitched battle
until betrayal's false note spoiled the tune.
To the enemy's chorus of jeers,
the Guardian faced his grisly death
with the same pride and courage
he'd led his life –
and ours.

Dead but not silenced,
for Wallace was more than a passing note
in the libretto of liberty
sung by so many Scots –
his was the very melody at its core;
a leitmotiv of patriotism
guaranteed,
even now,
to stir the blood
at the merest echo of his name
and have our hearts dancing.

Eulogy for William Wallace
written for Wallace Memorial Service
23 August 2005, London
Linda MacDonald-Lewis

*Linda MacDonald-Lewis of Oregon penned these lines last
year. She is engaged in spreading information about Scotland's
heritage and culture in the USA, both to those of Scottish
descent and others. The heading refers to the 'funeral' service
for Wallace in St Bartholomew the Great Church, London, on
the 700th anniversary of his death.*

Mourn now, weep on
my countrymen
for the man that stood,
steadfast to Passioned Principles
when few, if any would.

Call him giant, call him mad
or Sir, if you will,
The Wallace and his mighty sword
stirs the young hearts still.

He place his foot on freedom's path
walked it straight and wise
Then; in his wake; for all our sake
a Nation did arise.

Seven hundred years have passed
and now, we gather here
to honour him, who
gave so much
to that, which we hold dear.

Now . . . Respect is shown to Wallace
by all True Scots that could,
Standfast to Passioned Principles
when few, if any would.

Wallace

Andrew McCallum

*Andrew McCallum addresses Wallace with demotic familiarity
till in the last verse it becomes clear that the figure represents
a timeless and universal fighter against tyranny.*

Ye wur an awfu man!
A richt bother, in fact.
Ye an yer gang gaun
stravaigin owre the kintra,
fechtin the polis.

Aye, I weel mind the nicht
ye got intae a stour
ootside the Cross Keys.
Be richt they sud hae taen ye
then . . . but they didnae!

Naw . . . ye ay had the swick
o joukin in an oot,
landin a guid punch
then meltin ghaistlik awa
gin they cud catch ye.

There's bin mony a whap
twix then an noo in touns
up an doon the land,
some lang-minded, whiles ithers
are lang syne forgot.

And e'en tho yer body
has lang bin quartered tae
the warld's fowre corners,
ye're aften tae be seen still
fechtin the polis,

in Kashmir, Chechnya,
Iraq, Afghanistan,
Tiananmen Square...
tormentin tyrants a'where
wi yer muckle sword.

Wallace – Excerpts

Andrew Munro (unknown)

Wallace's fame and reputation crossed the Atlantic with Scottish emigrants. Andrew Munro of Brooklyn, New York viewed him with patriotic fervour, to such an extent that he wrote in verse his own version of the Wallace story over a period of 36 years. The task had started out as a competition with a friend but developed into a massive labour of love. He did not have access to the Hamilton text (though he had read it as a young man and refers to it disparagingly). His main source was a nineteenth century prose history, but he was probably also familiar with Jane Porter's highly romanticised account of Wallace in her 1810 volume, The Scottish Chieftains. *His hand-written volume, charmingly illustrated with his own watercolours, was bought by the Stirling Smith Art Gallery and Museum in 2005. His poetic talents are uneven, but he does have some memorable phrases, including his castigation of Wallace's betrayer, Sir John Menteith ('Thou soulless Scotch Iscariot'). He dwells on Wallace's romance. Here, however, is his paean to Wallace's heroic qualities and his zestful denunciation of Edward I ('Thou Nero of the British Isle') which ends his poem.*

'Twas he, whose aspiration high
   His country's banner had unfurl'd –
A banner brave that kiss'd the sky
In pure unsullied liberty,
   When Roman conqu'rors of the world
Invaded Caledonia's strand
   But fiercely from her bounds were hurl'd
A foil'd and disappointed band!

'Twas Wallace Wight! Immortal name!
The brightest on the page of fame!
'Twas Wallace! the brave patriot
Who to his country did devote
His godlike energies, and who
Nor toils nor dangers could subdue;
Nor Southern promises, nor gold
Could shake the firm and stedfast [sic] hold
His love on Scotland had, and, as
He through his life had been, so was
He when 'neath death he fell,
Brave, noble, incorruptible!
And while a noble gratitude
    Shall swell the breast and throb the heart
Of man for those who, unsubdued,
    By threats of death or tyrant's art,
    Have nobly acted patriot's part:
The name of Wallace shall rank high
Among the names that ne'er shall die!
And on through ages it shall be
A talisman for victory!

. . .

Then Wallace sheathes his sword in peace.
My hope is that as freeman I
Shall live, and as a freeman die,
Feeling, when death shall sound my knell,
That I have done my duty well.
Go, publish wide what I have spoken,
And never shall my word be broken.'

And thus he lived, until at last,
When eight more glorious years had pass'd –
Years which he to his country gave
In wisdom great and actions brave –
A Scottish traitor basely sold
The Wallace wight for English gold.

Oh, Edward! England's ruthless lord,
By me and each true Scot abhorr'd;
Debaser of thy country's coin; –
Thou tyrant o'er thy land and mine, –
Thou robber of that ancient stone
On which our kings were crown'd at Scone, –
Thou murd'rer of the Minstrel band
That cheer'd and nerv'd the Cambrian land, –
Thou who hast made poor Ireland feel
Upon her neck thine iron heel, –
Thief of the Templars' treasure thou, –
The brand of Cain is on thine brow, –
Was e'er thy face grac'd by a smile,
Thou Nero of the British Isle?
Thou liv'd'st a heartless homicide,
And a defeated dotard died.
The man, who had thy vengeance dar'd,
Thou could'st not bribe, yet him thou fear'd;
Yes him, whose patriotic zeal
    So nobly for his country wrought,
Thou, ignominious stoop'd to steal
    Because he never could be bought.
And as he liv'd, the patriot died,
His country's boast, his country's pride,

A martyr to earth's noblest cause –
His country's liberty and laws;
And while a Scotsman lives on earth,
And while the land that gave him birth
Exists, his memory shall go down
To endless ages with renown.

But thou, Menteith, accursed name,
Damn'd to eternal scorn and shame,
Thy trusting friend for English gold
Thou, fiendish, heartless traitor, sold;
Thy name's on hist'ry's page a blot,
Thou soulless Scotch Iscariot!

The Physical Diaspora of William Wallace

Les Murray

The distinguished Australian poet is very conscious of his Scottish roots. He writes, from New South Wales, that Wallace 'vouchsafed' him the lines below. In his poem, with characteristic originality, he counterpoises Wallace's legacy with the achievements of subsequent generations of Scots, including the worldwide Caledonian diaspora.

Your conquest of the world
by merchandrie and steam,
by logic and surgery
gets my sidelong esteem

but every true nation is
underlain by hard men.
I fought for a kingdom
to guard our ways in.

We'd fought off each other,
we'd fought off the Norse;
I chain-maced the English
from my wee shaggy horse

and my heart's near the Highlands,
my speen is in York,
one gnawed shin's in London,
my blood's in your talk –

such was their peace-work.
I confess I brought grue
down on cottars and lassies
but for less long than you

with your borderless realms
of doctrine and idea,
often colder than the cleavers
that sent me far and near,

me, followed by high-hearts,
the headlong and the poor
to Wembley and Calcutta,
to Melbourne and Bras d' Or

to be Scots for some lifetimes
and then Scots no more.

Last night I Googled William Wallace or 13 ways of looking at Wallace

Liz Niven

A Wallace poem for the internet age from Dumfries-based Liz Niven. Its random juxtapositions suggest various trains of thought, from the deep to the irreverent, about the Scots hero and his impact on the contemporary world. Liz Niven here writes in English but was joint winner of the James McCash Prize for Scots Poetry in 2003.

Five million websites,
more hits than the Battle of Falkirk

There's William Wallace, the Truth
And William Wallace, the Myth.
    William Wallace as Braveheart.
    Mel Gibson as William Wallace.

A man void of pity, a robber,
an arsonist and murderer.

William Wallace, the Hero, the Hammer,
The Highlander, The Hollywood Icon.

Sorry, but in truth William Wallace was a
complete and utter bastard of the 1st degree.

Buy William Wallace Garden Furniture
    in Ontario. Strong and sturdy.

Lady Diana is a modern William Wallace.
Her death, like Wallace's, might bring about
harmony and unity.

Nowadays, Wallace would be labelled as a UN
terrorist and bombed to buggery.

Visit the William Wallace pub in
Marleybone, London. We remember him
beheaded and dismembered.

William Wallace takes on Groundskeeper
Willie from the Simpsons.

The Truth behind the Man
(but the rest in Italian so I never found out)

Get William Wallace on Amazon
+ Free William Wallace Sheet Music.

Why not sell William Wallace on e-Bay?

Wallace's Lost Palace

Rosaleen Orr

*Rosaleen Orr lives in Kilbarchan, Renfrewshire, quite close to
Elderslie, and is a painter. She won joint first prize in the James
McCash Prize for Scots Poetry in 2003 and employs familiar,
conversational Scots to make her – often serious – points.*

Here's tae ye Big Man
Ah raise ma charged quaich tae ye Sur
Hero of here aboot near me in Renfrewshire
Wur ye as rerr an' big as they say?
Yir supposed tae hiv hefted a broadsword
Higher nur ma man's heid
Fegs size isnae everythin' indeed
Money a wee Bantam guy
Fought fur Scotland's freedom anaw
We'll let that wee fly stick tae the waw

Okay then big gallus hero
Oor younkers hardly know yir name
Wis it Mel Gibson or Liam Neeson
Brocht ye yir oor o' pictorial fame?
Mediaeval Che Guevara
Tholed his death in monstrous pain
General an' man o' parts
Loved humanity loved the arts
We couldnae hing oan tae his Elderslie Palace
Hearts o' Scotland feel the shame!

Massive Hero

Rosaleen Orr

Massive hero wield yir broadsword
Scare the guys at Holyrood
Ither nations vaunt their heroes
Take the steps o' the wise and good
William Wallace ye inspired yer warriors
Tae roust the Southreners back tae thur hame
We'll keep oor sojers within oor borders
Wallace we'll learn yir patriot's game
Let thae southreners mak thur policies
Gie us leave tae mak wur ain
Scare oor leaders Wullie Wallace
Gar them fearter o' you nur they ur o' Blair
Gie thum nightmares second sight mares
Gonnae get the southreners oota wur hair?

Bonny Watter

Janet Paisley

Janet Paisley is a poet, playwright and scriptwriter with a series of admired poetry collections to her name, in English and in Scots. Here she employs Scots. Her first little poem records a meeting between Wallace and Robert the Bruce on opposite banks of the Bonny Water near Bonnybridge. The second seems to chide Wallace for acting, as he did in 1297, in the name of John Balliol rather than for freedom itself.

a wee dreiple ower stane
atween twa men bit yin
wad be gut tormentit,
the ither, tormentit king.

did thur lugs haud bird-sang,
green ur grey clood thur een,
wis it teemin wi a rainbow
ahint haar, a brichter sun.

wad they ken the wey furrit,
yin speired like he micht
aside guid clear cauld watter,
did thon day birl fae nicht.

Film Fur Ye

Janet Paisley

Scots gied ower thair richt
tae yon majesty next door,
couldnae mak up thair minds,
thae'd bin slicht pickin afore
sae naebody wis dumfounert
when Ed haun-picked a whore.

A croon's an awfy scunner,
it maks ye gie a damn.
At least, it did wi Balliol
wha stertit thinkin, king I am.
Eddie, mair'n a mite tee'd aff,
ordert the Tower fur yon bam.

Naebody reckoned Wallace
tae he cried 'noo hing oan, Ed,
it's up tae us wha's king'
richt contrair tae whit'd been said.
Wi nae reason an worse rhyme
he turnt the hale thing oan it's head.

A peety tae be laudit
fur whit ye didnae dae,
tae cry it wis fur freedom,
whit Bruce won, an no fur lealty
tae thon toom jaiket mannie
Jock turnt oot no tae be.

Wallace in Lanark

Andrew Philip

Andrew Philip was commissioned by BBC Scotland to write a modern version of a key moment in the Wallace story for part of a programme on Radio Scotland to mark the 700th anniversary of Wallace's death. Here he tells the story of Wallace's doomed romance in Lanark and of the retribution he visited on the Sheriff of Lanark and the 'Southrons.' The language is Scots but with a deliberate raciness to appeal to a contemporary audience of schoolchildren.

There wis a lassie lived in Lanark toun.
She wis a bonnie craitur, douce an canny,
but she steyed by her lane, 'cause she'd nae faimly
although she couldnae be much ower eighteen.
Her faither an her mither had baith deed
a few year syne, but that wis juist the stairt
o aw her wae: the English broke her hairt
when they killt her only brither in cauld bluid
an Hazelrig, the sheriff they'd installed,
had got it in his heid that she shuid wed
his son—a scheme that ony Scottish lass wid dread.
She kept her hous as quait 's she cuid an called
on Edward for tae buy fae him protection
fae onything his men wid dae in war.
Wan day in Lanark, Wallace spotted her
as she gaed tae the kirk for her confession.
As soon 's he seen her, his hairt wis tint:
Wallace was in love. His mind wis torn in twae:
wan hauf o him wis ettlin for tae gae
back tae battle; the ither hauf had funt

awthing that it needed tae be happy.
He tried tae puit her oot his heid throu fechts
wi Southron sodgers stationed in the west,
but couldnae juist forget sae braw a lassie.
Syne weddin bells wis heard throu Lanark toun;
a bride an groom as blythe as ony ither
stepped oot the kirk tae stairt their life thegither,
but Hazelrig sat in his hous an fumed.
Wallace an his wife soon had a wean,
a lassie juist as bonnie as her mammy,
an Wallace kept hissel awa fae rammies
wi Englishmen, but the sheriff hatched a plan
thegither wi a knight cried Robert Thorn.
Wallace an his men they wanted deid;
the plan wis tae surroun them in the street
at some pynt when they thocht they'd be unairmed.
Sir John Grahame, that wis hardy, wise an leal,
cam tae Lanark as he'd done afore
wi fifteen fechtin men tae see for shair
that Wallace, wife an wean wis keepin weil.
Thir twa went tae mass wi aw their men
decked oot in the season's fantoosh green.
As they left the kirk when mass wis duin,
the strangest cheil amang the Englishmen
began tae lichtly Wallace an his sqaud;
his salutation, nocht but scorn:
'Greetings! Good day! Bon senjor and good morning!'
'Wha learnt you?' speired Wallace. 'Whae're you tauntin?'
'Why sir,' he said, 'ain't you from overseas?
Then pardon me. You seemed to us to be
an embassy sent by a foreign queen.'
'Whit pairdon's oors tae grant, ye will be gied.'
'As you're Scots, you'll get your greeting yet:

Ock eye the noo, big man, and bannock let!'
Mair Englishmen wis gaitherin in the street
an Wallace wis fell laith tae stairt a fecht.
Wan Southron snashed an pued at his lang sword.
'Haud still yer haun,' said Wallace, 'an yaise words.'
'With your long sword you pose a mighty threat.'
'Yer wumman didnae say much aboot that.'
'What cause d'you have to wear that bright green garb?'
'Ma cause is maistly juist tae mak ye radge.'
'What should a Scot do with so fine a knife?'
'Sae said the priest that last shamed yer ain wife.
Yon wumman's served him weil an served him lang
while his wean grew up as your heir an son.'
'Summink tells me all your talk is scorn.'
'Yer maw wis tricked afore ye were born.'
The force that wis assembled roon them syne
wis fu twa hunner—stalwart, brave an strang.
The Scots seen whit wis headed for their band:
Hazelrig an Thorn aye close at haun,
the multitude wi weapons burnished weil.
The worthy Scots, that aw wis bold an fell,
gied the English sodgers sic braw dunts
their Saxon bluid went skirpin ower the grund.
Wallace, fechtin feircely in amang them,
smat the richt haun aff a Southron.
When yon boy funt that he cuid fecht
nae mair, he held his sheild up wi his left,
syne oot his stump o airm he slaistered
buckets o bluid in Wallace's face, whaur
it got intae his een an skaed his sicht.
Sir John syne gied the English boy a richt
strang blow wi his guid sword; in rage
he sent the Southron skitin til his grave.

The danger wis that frichtsome, haird an strang.
The rammy lasted unco lang.
The Englishmen wis gaitherin awfae fast.
The worthy Scots cuid leave the street at last
when mony Englishmen wis slain an wounded.
The Scots aw made their wey tae Wallace
defendin theirsels richt weil.
Wallace an Sir John, wi braw stiff steel,
steyed back until their men had raxed the gate.
His wife, that wi despair wis gey near gyte,
seen the danger, heard the awfae din,
opened the gate an let the Scots aw in.
They quit the place an on they gaed
tae safety. Fifty Englishmen lay deid.
The bonnie wife did awthing in her micht
tae haud the English back wi cannie slicht
while Wallace an his men made for the wuids
an on tae Cartlin Craggs as fast 's they cuid.
But when the Southrons seen he had escaped
they taen his wife an syne puit her tae daith,
Whit wey they done it, that I dinnae ken.
On siclike things I hae nae time tae dwell.
When Wallace heard whit Hazelrig had done
the pair man gey near tummelt tae the grund.
His force set oot for Lanark wi aw speed.
The watchmen o the toun peyed little heed.
The Scots split up: the company that went in
wi guid Sir John eidently huntin
for Robert Thorn, while Wallace an his men
fuint Hazelrig lyin in his bed.
Wi wan kick, Wallace broke the thick door doun.
Hazelrig sat up. 'Who's making all that din?'
he speired. 'Wallace, that ye've socht aw day.
The woman's deid, an you, by God, will pey.'

The sheriff kent this wis nae time tae laze.
Syne he sprang up an tried tae quit the place.
The nicht wis mirk, but Wallace seen him move.
The lang, shairp sword wis clappit in his neive.
As Hazelrig cam at him in a fash,
Wallace smashed his blade throu bane an flesh
an sent him heelstergowdie ower the stair.
Auchinleck o Gilbank wisnae shair
that Hazelrig wis deid, an thrust
a dagger three times in the sheriff's breist.
The skraich o battle skirled aboot the street
an mony fowk wis trampled unnerfuit.
Young Hazelrig met Wallace face tae face
an bold Sir William felled him wi wan straik.
A fair few fowk they slew in Lanark toun,
that aw wis feart wi hideous noise an din.
Some loupit stairs an some wis steikit ben.
Sir John Grahame an his men set aflame
the hous whaur Robert Thorn wis left
tae be consumed by fire baith bane an flesh.
Twa hunner fowerty Englishmen wis slain
but priests an weeminfowk they let alane.
Thir fowk they left tae gae their wey next mornin
wi naething but their claes an shoon, in murnin.
When ither Scots got wind o this braw news
fae ivry pairt o Scotlan syne they drew
tae Wallace for tae settle in the toun
that wis aye theirs by richt. Thus Wallace won
some pairts o Scotlan back fae Southron bands
by dint o his ain strenth an stalwart hauns.
The Scots that, roon the Wallace, cam thegither
waled him as their chief, chieftain and leader.

Song Book

Alison Prince

Arran-based Alison Prince is an award-winning children's author as well as a writer of poetry for adults. She recalls here how her parents passed on a sense of Scottish inheritance to their family, though they were based in London.

Myths filled the London semi,
and the smells of washing and Scotch broth.
He'd come for work and found it, slowly grown
into the Bank as young feet fill their shoes,
uncomfortably. But he made no fuss.

His wife would have complained, but knew
there was no point. She missed
the cobbles of Dundee, the ships, the run
of East-coast voices. She was not
willing to join the local tennis club.

On the piano with the stacks of Bach,
Beethoven, Schubert, that he played each night
for some small solace, was
the Scottish Students' Song Book
with its cover dropping off.

A man draped in a toga played a lyre
as the sun set, and in the sky it said,
GAUDEAMUS IGITUR,
JUVENES DUM SUMUS.
Let us sing praises while we are still young.

The young ones of the house
stood open-beaked about this music-nest,
singing like fledglings. *Ae Fond Kiss,*
Ye Banks and Braes, Green Grow
the Rashes-O,

and, when their father turned
to National Anthems, *Scots*
Wha' Hae Wi' Wallace Bled.
Children who sing of blood think with the heart,
not with the head.

Nobody said
who this man was, no history
pinned him in true event. He stayed
a blood-deep thing, a secret fire
of passion and regret.

The child who took her mother's hand
when they began that song
followed her sense of loss
back to the hills and islands,
listening.

Songs echo on, and battle cries
rise from the terraces. A thought brings pain.
Wallace now would be an MSP.
And/or a football fan.
Her hands are old. They close on myth and dream.

Seven Hundred Years

Alan Reid

These straightforward but perceptive verses speculate about Wallace's thoughts in his last hours. They have a feeling of authenticity.

And how did you go to your death?
Did you hold the martyr's defiance that our fathers
    proudly told,
Or did you scream for mercy at the butcher's cut:
A mortal man on the edge of the abyss?

Where were your thoughts that final day?
Did you drift homewards,
Clinging to the last images of the land you held so dear,
Or did you mind your days of learning and struggle above
    the noise
To place your soul in the hands of a higher judgment?

And how did the eyes of London see your passing?
Did they hate you as a traitor and a killer of priests and
    bairns,
Revelling in the justice of your spilling blood?
Surely there were those clutching their own breasts
As the beating heart was torn from your frame,
Dwelling on the thinnest thread that held their earthly life.

Perhaps it was still hatred you clung to,
A rage to dull the pain until the merciful axe fell.
To have met them to their beards –
Had that not been enough for one man and one life time;
Cressingham's bloated corpse consolation for your own?

Or was it Falkirk's Field and failure that haunted your
    dying thoughts,
In a despair that cried 'All for nought' – the fight is lost!
So courage does not prevail over steel and gold, fear and
    greed.
Were doubt and terror your only companions at
    Smithfield?

Can we honour such a man in stone and words alone –
In poetry and film?
A man of deeds and courage lives on in deeds and courage
Or not at all.
To live meekly by the rule of another shames us all
And shames us still.

The Towering Wallace

Marian Reid

There are towers named after Wallace scattered through Scotland, as well as natural features such as woods and wells and burns, all showing the grip he has on his country-men's imagination. Marian Reid's word play in her title about this towering figure of Scottish history is neatly echoed in her last line.

I'm standing here, looking up,
Heeled at the Wallace Tower,
A totem on High Street, Ayr.
Traffic is swirling around me –
Tourists, buses and shoppers.

Miles to the north, long ago,
A freedom fighter was born,
Young William vowed to restore
Scotland to national glory.
His story of life remains misty…

But do not be mistaken. His end
Was a definite document
Sly shifting of sides – Betrayal!
A brutal hanging in London,
A life given bravely, for country.

A Knight with an army of sorts,
He fought a cat-and-mouse battle,
In Ayrshire, on its dip and slope,
Across Scotland, for its liberty.
His cause, alone, never wavered.

His good strong arm with its sword
Rises above us, high on the Tower,
A presence still felt. Local hero.
Crowds follow on, walk beneath
The stature of tall William Wallace.

Wallace Triptych

Alan Riach

The Professor of Scottish Literature at Glasgow University is himself a poet as well as academic, with several published collections. His triptych showing three aspects of Wallace does not dodge the negative side of the Scottish hero; the first panel, as it were, depicting Wallace's decision to have the English leader Cressingham skinned after the battle of Stirling Bridge – 'a cruelty, required?' Then he compares Wallace with Burns as a champion of the common man. Wallace himself speaks in the third panel, pledging himself to make 'this shilpit nation' complete and fit to speak to others independently.

1. After the Battle

Wallace knelt down, before the bleeding man.
The salt grass brushed his calves.

The dying man looked up at him, eyes
keen. Proximity
                Was everything.
Wallace let his left hand steady himself, fingers
outstretched, fingertips / on the earth
between the grassblades.

The English eyes turned round to him, afraid.
Wallace had seen them already, started to

wipe his fingers on the grass, forgiving
and condemning in that touch.

Compassion for all
Quislings
gone.

What I care about now,
                    is not to do with this
(ice in the hand of winter, mind elemental snow)
No. Nor can it be more abstract.
            (Language, life, a world more full
            of what there is than all that
            I could learn)
No. What I care about now,
he said, is what I can do,
what I can do for this good.
            The border is there, and needed.
            And we want none of you.
                    He rose and turned,
into a seam of sunlight on the hills.
'Skin him', he said.
            There is, this –
a cruelty, required?
Decisively.

II. Abstract

It is the fact they had to make him *Sir*
He was common. He was
of the people.

And then the passion in those learned hands
grasped on the handle,
swinging that sword.

That there might be room for us to be
in all the creativity
we need.

And all the men and women in the country
might have the words and air
to breathe their lives in.

He stands as Burns, or Democrats, always stand, *for*
correction of the folly and the false,
to kill the aristocracy

and end the farce of that enforced distinction
always. The lifting of the head.
The honesty.

III. At Stirling Brig

This shilpit nation, set against itself
I'll make complete, and fit to speak to others
independently.
      Rax me the hilt o' that sword!
Whit sang is this?

His hearing took the sounds
of languages and music in cathedrals, voices raised
to magnify by stone. He nodded and approved,
his muscle tensing, knowledge of the prospect bringing
fear and resolution. *People of Scotland, now.*

     And nimbleness, the unpredicted element.
The form of church and righteousness /
the variedness of folk, and words.

These things are brought to this:
Wallace on horse, the spearsmen
ready. Blood crusted on the blades.

The bridge. The water running. Brightness.
The prospect.

Election Day

Donald Smith

Donald Smith writes his poem from the vantage point of Stirling Castle, at the epicentre of the struggle for Scottish independence, and explores his own perspectives on Wallace and Bruce, the past and the present, on a day of democratic choice.

William Wallace, you are not my hero,
but I recognise your stubborn
guardianship, the resistance call,
when leaders of our realm
deserted their community.
Robert Bruce, you are not my hero,
though I acknowledge your resolve,
the steely cunning, your endurance
and the will to power that armed you
for victory and the wounds of kingship.
Standing on the castle rock
above Stirling Bridge and Bannockburn,
summoned to account
by convocation of the hills,
while through the Lomond Gap,
the narrow defiles of the Allan,
the broadening flats of Stirling Carse,
rivers and roads conjoin,
I face my question.
This is the navel and the omphalos:
history's diverse footprints coalesce

and people of the present,
immigrant and emigrant all
become joint owners of the future.
What says the oracle?
'I am your elective freedom,
and the burden of your choice.'

Excerpts from **The Wallace**

Sydney Goodsir Smith (1915 – 1975)

Sydney Goodsir Smith's play The Wallace *was staged as part of the official Edinburgh International Festival in 1960. Goodsir Smith, a New Zealander by birth but of Scottish background, was a highly regarded poet, critic, and artist. These three extracts from his play show the hardening of Wallace's resolve after the murder of his wife; his final eloquent confrontation with Edward I at his trial in the Great Hall of Westminster; and his regard for the common man Goodsir Smith may have taken liberties with known historical facts in the climactic scene, but to excellent dramatic effect.*

Wallace is driven to fight by the murder of his wife Marian, whom Goodsir Smith called Mirren

WALLACE
. . . Nae quarter shall we gie, nae pitie shaw –
For her sake there shall then thousand dee,
And I, Murray, insatiate o' bluid
Till this skaith is healed that's opened
In me nou, gowpin wide – ah, Mirren! –
Bluid will hae bluid, indeed, or vengeance'
Drouth is slockenit in Wallace –

MURRAY
Wallace, put the harness on your rage
And bend it for our purpose – This is a sign
Frae God, auld friend, to mettle us –

WALLACE
Guid Murray, ay, maybe ye're richt.
I'd liefer hae nae sign and her alive,
But God has willed it sae, it seems,
That a frail lassie's daith shoud gie barb
And spur til bluidie vengeance, war
Sleepless and pitiless. We'll greit
Nae mair, but cry up daith and fire,
Destruction! Ah, Mirren! Here was
The maist beauteous flouer o' the flock,
Here was my luve, here Scotland
Incarnate, the White Rose breathin
In a lassie's form, cauld nou and spreitless,
But a queen, laurelled wi her daith
And wi her ain reid bluid anointit –
A fell sacrifice to bless a war.
No, she isna deid, but lives in me,
To airm my bluidie hand, and skail
Aa mercie frae the hairt wi the great
Storm o' her sillie daith. I am
Become a priest, Murray, a dedicate
Wi ae crusade – deliverance!

*He picks up the clout stained
with* MIRREN's *bluid.*

This, sweet-hairt, will be our gonfalon
And standart, aye in the van o' battle,
First to view wir victories and last
To leave defeat. Vengeance is mine,
Saith the Lord – and sae says Wallace wicht!
Nou, haste ye, Murray, til the Craigs.
We hae work the morn.

Wallace addresses Edward I at his trial

WALLACE
. . . This is nocht the daith of Wallace, Edward,
Nor yet the end of Scotland, in your
Menteith-peace, or desert-conquest either,
But the birth-thraws of its glorie and its
Triumph. Scotland has wan, my lord, and you,
Nane ither, gied us victorie...

KING EDWARD
Ha!

Murmurs.

WALLACE
Through this lang war, echt year o' fire and sword
And famine, greit and bluid and daith,
Ye've made a nation, sir. Hammer
O' the Scots indeed! By the Rood,
Ye're richter nor ye ken. Ye've hammerit
A nation intil life, ennobled it,
And held it up like a banner til aa men
For evermair – a standart o' the pride
And independence of a folk whase sperit's
Free and winna bou til thirldom ever –
No for land or treisure, consequence
Or pouer, but for ae thing that, wanting,
Leas life wersh and thowless, dozent,
Meaningless; but, possess't, lets man stand
Upricht in the likeness of his God
That made him sae: Freedom! Ay, thirldom
Is the soul in chains – e'en in the mid o' plenty,

As libertie is the soul at lairge – though
It be in puirtith and defeat. This we hae wan.
For aa this, Edward, I, in the name o' Scotland,
First o' the nations, thank ye, for your gift
Til aa humanitie. *You* should be vauntie,
Sir! Put aff yon dowie look! Your
Immortalitie is in sauf keep, juist
As ye said, SCOTORUM MALLEUS...

Wallace on the Scottish People

In the end, my friends,
We've nane but the folk; they've nocht
To loss but life and libertie.
But gin we've them, we've aa. They're Scotland,
Nane ither. The pouer of e'en the greatest lord,
Like Bruce, is nocht in the end but the folk
He leads. They micht be beat in battle,
Slain in thousands, conquered and thirlit –
But no for aye. Spring maun follow winter.
The Romans cam and gaed. Sae will Edward.
Ah, Alexander, come again!

1305

Geddes Thomson (1939–2002)

A poem in the words of Wallace, the hunted man – thought-provoking and philosophically rather bleak, though with vivid imagery.

On a lonely hill,
A bare brown hill,
I met a lonely wolf.
We looked into
Each other's eyes
With utter weariness.
The hunted and the hunted.

They say the land
Was green with trees,
Alive with wolves,
Even on the high hills.
Once.

Trees, wolves, men;
These can be destroyed.

Ideas are not different.

When I am taken
Do not blame the traitor
Or think that English gold
Has bought my body.

Do not, like the priests,
Elevate the idea
Above the people.

Question rather the idea.

When you see
My severed head
Spiked above a bridge
To terrify our people,
Do not think
It is not my head
Or that the soul
Has left the body, safely,
Like a little lark
Soaring to heaven.
Remember, rather,
That the bird returns
To earth, always.

The Wallace Breakfast

Hamish Whyte

Hamish Whyte's imaginary Wallace breakfast with its lumpy porridge, stale bread, and wersh water, is indeed a sour feast with a macabre dance to follow. Is Whyte criticising Scotland's neglect of its martyred hero?

Visit Scotland!
Join the Scots in celebrating their country's greatest son
who fought for freedom.
Every 23rd of August Scots join together
to remember William Wallace
on the anniversary of his cruel death
in 1305.
They eat a breakfast of lumpy porridge,
stale bread and wersh water.
They recite long passages from Blind Harry's *Wallace*
in the translation by William Hamilton
and, echoing Wallace's words before the Battle of Falkirk –
'I have brought you to the ring – now dance if you can' –
they form a circle and dance round five times
in honour of the number of pieces
his body was chopped into at his execution,
singing:

> an arm for Perth
> a leg for Berwick
> an arm for Stirling
> a leg for Newcastle
> who knows where his trunk went
> but his spirit lives for ever!

'A Scottish Prejudice . . .'

Rab Wilson

Rab Wilson draws for his title on Burns's comment about the profound influence of Wallace on his feelings for Scotland. Sanquhar-based Wilson, a former mining engineer, now psychiatric nurse as well as poet, here offers a vigorous autobiographic account of his own initiation into the Wallace story.

In ma bairntid, i' the primary schuil,
Ah coudnae thole arithmetic lessons;
Fractions, lang diveesions an gaes-in-taes.
Thair *'Language Laboratory'* let me cauld,
Aye trailin ahint twa, three smairt lassies,
Wha aye struck gowd when as wis left wae bronze.
In a scunner ah wid longingly gaze
Oot the windae at promised Summer hills,
Cled in trees tae be clomb, burns tae be swum.
But aye an oan ah'd sit there in a dwam,
When Mrs MacSween wove magical spells,
Anent Scotia's fecht fir independence;
Hou the bold Douglas sclimb't up Embra's crags,
An ding't the hale English garrison doun,
Hou the Bruce oan a fleet hielant powny
Cleaved rash de Valence's prood helm in twa,
An William Wallace, brave-heartit Wallace!
Each gory detail o his obscene daith
Wis etched upon our young an fertile minds;
The noble heid, pykt atour London Bridge,
His airms displayed at Berwick an the Tyne,
The legs, hung out lik butcher's bluidy jynts,

At Aiberdeen an Perth, abune the ports,
Fir rattans, hoodie craws an laithsome mauchs
Tae swall their kytes an feast theirsels upon.
The kindae mundane horror weans enjoy!
Nou mair as thirty year syne ah sit here,
A copy o *'Blin Harry'* i' ma haun,
Readin the notes o some auld Scots divine,
Jamieson, quotin frae Andrew de Wyntown;
'*A thousand thre hundyr and the fyft yhere*
Eftyr the byrth of oure Lord dere,
Schyre Jhon of Menteth in tha days
Tuk in Glasgw Williame Walays,
And send hym in-til Ingland swne,
Thare wes he quartaryd and wndwne
Be despyte and hat inwy:
Thare he tholyd this martyry.'

Micht thon auld teacher wryly smile tae ken,
The boys she tocht hae aa nou grown Scots men,
An thon keen prejudice whilk kennled Burns
Whilk she sae glegly instillt intae us,
Strivin tae mak siccar, lest we forget,
Still floods *our* veins, an *nevvir* will abate.

Author's Notes

In his famous autobiographical letter to John Moore, Scotland's National Poet, Robert Burns, described his recognition of his feelings for Scotland: '. . . the story of William Wallace poured a Scottish prejudice in my veins which will boil along there till the flood-gates of life shut in eternal rest.'

Some other books published by **LUATH** PRESS

Blind Harry's Wallace

William Hamilton of Gilbertfield
Introduced by Elspeth King
ISBN 0 946487 33 2 PBK £8.99

The original story of the real braveheart, Sir William Wallace. Racy, blood on every page, violently anglophobic, grossly embellished, vulgar and disgusting, clumsy and stilted, a literary failure, a great epic. Whatever the verdict on BLIND HARRY, this is the book which has done more than any other to frame the notion of Scotland's national identity. Despite its numerous 'historical inaccuracies', it remains the principal source for what we now know about the life of Wallace.

The novel and film *Braveheart* were based on the 1722 Hamilton edition of this epic poem. Burns, Wordsworth, Byron and others were greatly influenced by this version 'wherein the old obsolete words are rendered more intelligible', which is said to be the book, next to the Bible, most commonly found in Scottish households in the eighteenth century. Burns even admits to having 'borrowed... a couplet worthy of Homer' directly from Hamilton's version of BLIND HARRY to include in 'Scots wha hae'.

Elspeth King, in her introduction to this, the first accessible edition of BLIND HARRY in verse form since 1859, draws parallels between the situation in Scotland at the time of Wallace and that in Bosnia and Chechnya in the 1990s. Seven hundred years to the day after the Battle of Stirling Bridge, the 'Settled Will of the Scottish People' was expressed in the devolution referendum of 11 September 1997. She describes this as a landmark opportunity for mature reflection on how the nation has been shaped, and sees BLIND HARRY'S WALLACE as an essential and compelling text for this purpose.

On the Trail of William Wallace

David R. Ross
ISBN 0 946487 47 2 PBK £7.99

How close to reality was *Braveheart*?
Where was Wallace actually born?
What was the relationship between Wallace and Bruce?
Are there any surviving eye-witness accounts of Wallace?
How does Wallace influence the psyche of today's Scots?

On the Trail of William Wallace offers a refreshing insight into the life and heritage of the great Scots hero whose proud story is at the very heart of what it means to be Scottish. Not concentrating simply on the hard historical facts of Wallace's life, the book also takes into account the real significance of Wallace and his effect on the ordinary Scot through the ages, manifested in the many sites where his memory is marked.

In trying to piece together the jigsaw of the reality of Wallace's life, David Ross weaves a subtle flow of new information with his own observations. His engaging, thoughtful and at times amusing narrative reads with the ease of a historical novel, complete with all the intrigue, treachery and romance required to hold the attention of the casual reader and still entice the more knowledgable historian.

74 places to visit in Scotland and the north of England
One general map and 3 location maps
Stirling and Falkirk battle plans
Wallace's route through London
Chapter on Wallace connections in North America and elsewhere
Reproductions of rarely seen illustrations

On the Trail of William Wallace will be enjoyed by anyone with an interest in Scotland, from the passing tourist to the most fervent nationalist. It is an encyclopaedia-cum-guide book, literally stuffed with fascinating titbits not usually on offer in the conventional history book.

Braveheart: From Hollywood to Holyrood

Lin Anderson
ISBN 1 84282 066 4 PBK £7.99

Braveheart was the best movie of 1995, winning 5 Oscars and re-establishing the historical epic as a film genre, paving the way for the successes of *Gladiator* and *Lord of the Rings* that followed.

Braveheart reached a global audience with its powerful re-telling of the almost forgotten story of William Wallace and his struggle to defend Scotland's freedom. Described as 'the most politically influential movie of the 20th century', it also had a part to play in the political change that swept Scotland, mobilising public opinion to aid the return of a Scottish Parliament after a gap of 300 years.

Braveheart: From Hollywood to Holyrood is the first book about this movie phenomenon, discussing the life and legacy of William Wallace through the modern image of the hero as presented in the film. Written with the co-operation of Randall Wallace, author of the screenplay and novelisation of *Braveheart*, and including never before published photographs, this is the long-awaited handbook for *Braveheart* fans around the world.

Luath Press Limited

committed to publishing well written books worth reading

LUATH PRESS takes its name from Robert Burns, whose little collie Luath
(*Gael.*, swift or nimble) tripped up Jean Armour at a wedding and gave him
the chance to speak to the woman who was to be his wife and the
abiding love of his life. Burns called one of *The Twa Dogs*
Luath after Cuchullin's hunting dog in *Ossian's Fingal*.
Luath Press was established in 1981 in the heart of
Burns country, and is now based a few steps up the
road from Burns' first lodgings on Edinburgh's
Royal Mile.
Luath offers you distinctive writing with a hint of
unexpected pleasures.

Most bookshops in the UK, the US, Canada, Aus-
tralia, New Zealand and parts of Europe either carry
our books in stock or can order them for you. To order
direct from us, please send a £sterling cheque, postal
order, international money order or your credit card details
(number, address of cardholder and expiry date) to us at
the address below. Please add post and packing as follows:
UK – £1.00 per delivery address; overseas surface mail – £2.50 per delivery
address; overseas airmail – £3.50 for the first book to each delivery address,
plus £1.00 for each additional book by airmail to the same address. If your
order is a gift, we will happily enclose your card or message at no extra charge.

Luath Press Limited
543/2 Castlehill
The Royal Mile
Edinburgh EH1 2ND
Scotland
Telephone: 0131 225 4326 (24 hours)
Fax: 0131 225 4324
email: gavin.macdougall@luath.co.uk
Website: www.luath.co.uk